OFF THE MAIN ROAD
— REVISITED —
San Vicente & Barona

For Geoff & Sherry
with best regards
Claud Jennegan
Sept 2013

DEDICATION

The author has been twice blessed by two loving and supportive wives. This book is dedicated to them both. First, to Nancy, whom we lost after 51 happy years of marriage. She was an avid reader and an inspiration for the original "Off the Main Road." She was the mainstay in that first effort to produce a history book in 1983.

Betty and I were married in 2001. She's not only been my loving partner in marriage, but an active supporter of our community. Over time, it's become clear that this first book about our valley needed to be "revisited." Betty's encouragement and help in its creation and promotion have been invaluable.

OFF THE MAIN ROAD
— REVISITED —
San Vicente & Barona

A history of those who shaped events in the

RANCHO CAÑADA de SAN VICENTE y
MESA del PADRE BARONA

By

CHARLES R. LeMENAGER

"Revisited" Edition – May 2013

ISBN-13: 978-1489522849

Printed in the United States of America

Published by
Eagle Peak Publishing Company
P.O. Box 1283
Ramona, California 92065

Cover design by Ernest Prinzhorn

OFF THE MAIN ROAD
— REVISITED —
San Vicente & Barona

CONTENTS

FOREWARD

The author first saw the San Vicente and Barona Rancho valleys in April 1970. There were five families living in San Vicente's main northern valleys plus the small community of 20 families in Little Klondike. The Barona Indian Reservation, covering most of the southern part of the rancho, was home to about 325 Mission Indians. Cattle were still grazing in those two main sectors. Dorace Scarbery was running his Polled Hereford breed in the north San Vicente area and the Banegas, Phoenix and Quitac families were running their herds on the reservation on open range. The total area to which this book refers is contained within the boundaries of the 13,316-acre Mexican land grant, "Rancho Cañada de San Vicente y Mesa del Padre Barona," established in 1845.

Not many cattle graze freely in these valleys anymore. Dramatic changes have taken place in those four decades. They took place mainly because of two dynamics. A strong developer with vision bought 3,250 acres of San Vicente's northern valleys and developed a large planned community called San Diego Country Estates. While in the southern part of the rancho, legalized gaming was established on the Barona Indian Reservation.

As in the past, whenever my corporate duties moved me to a new place, my wife Nancy and I would search library shelves for any information we could find about our new home. The results of our quest when coming to Ramona were disappointing. While several books and pamphlets have been published about the ranchos of San Diego County, only a few pages in any of them were devoted to the San Vicente and Barona Rancho. In some cases, details presented turn out to be in error.

It had been a long-standing ambition of mine to write a serious history someday. I put my new Ramona home down in the back of my mind as being the prime candidate for such an effort, and started doing research for this book shortly after getting settled.

The evolution of two distinctive and diverse societies on this same backcountry land makes for interesting history. And as interesting history indeed took place before I first wrote about this area in 1983, the following years have been just as fascinating.

Life for the Barona Indians has been transformed from economically lean to comfortably affluent. Expensive new homes have been springing up all over the reservation. Educational and social infrastructure has been added, vastly improving life for the typical Barona family.

The master-planned new community of San Diego Country Estates has been built out to the limit of its approved development plan with approximately 10,000 people now residing there. Many new families have moved in since we first published this history. To ignore the dynamic changes taking place over the past 30 years is to ignore important local history. This is an attempt to catch up on some of those happenings.

We hope you find the book interesting and derive a fraction of the enjoyment in reading it that we had in bringing it to you.

San Vicente Valley
San Diego County, California
May 2013
C.R.L.

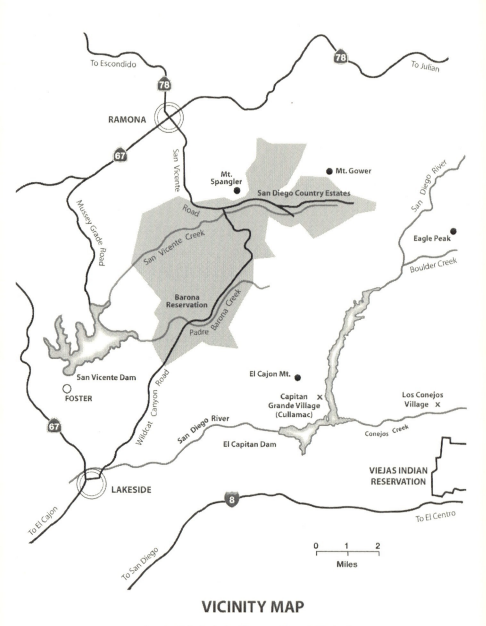

VICINITY MAP

▨ Rancho Cañada de San Vicente y Mesa del Padre Barona

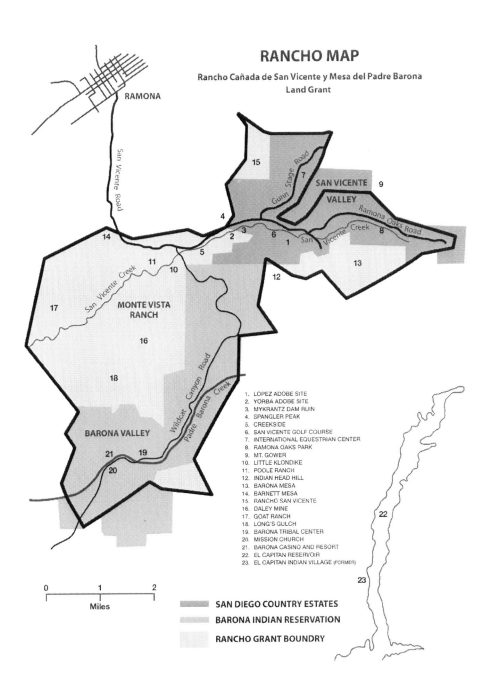

RANCHO MAP

Rancho Cañada de San Vicente y Mesa del Padre Barona
Land Grant

RAMONA

San Vicente Road

15

Stage Road

Gunn

7

SAN VICENTE 9

VALLEY

Ramona Oaks Road

4

14

2 3

6

1

San Vicente Creek

8

5

11

10

San Vicente Creek

13

12

17

MONTE VISTA
RANCH

16

18

Wildcat Canyon Road

Padre Barona Creek

BARONA VALLEY

21   19

20

1. LOPEZ ADOBE SITE
2. YORBA ADOBE SITE
3. MYKRANTZ DAM RUIN
4. SPANGLER PEAK
5. CREEKSIDE
6. SAN VICENTE GOLF COURSE
7. INTERNATIONAL EQUESTRIAN CENTER
8. RAMONA OAKS PARK
9. MT. GOWER
10. LITTLE KLONDIKE
11. POOLE RANCH
12. INDIAN HEAD HILL
13. BARONA MESA
14. BARNETT MESA
15. RANCHO SAN VICENTE
16. DALEY MINE
17. GOAT RANCH
18. LONG'S GULCH
19. BARONA TRIBAL CENTER
20. MISSION CHURCH
21. BARONA CASINO AND RESORT
22. EL CAPITAN RESERVOIR
23. EL CAPITAN INDIAN VILLAGE (FORMER)

22

23

0   1   2

Miles

■ **SAN DIEGO COUNTRY ESTATES**

■ **BARONA INDIAN RESERVATION**

■ **RANCHO GRANT BOUNDRY**

EAGLE PEAK as viewed from San Vicente Valley. Mt. Cuyamaca is in the background and the San Diego Country Estates tennis condominiums are in the foreground.

The Setting

THE "RANCHO CAÑADA de San Vicente y Mesa del Padre Barona" became a geopolitical entity in 1846 when the last Mexican governor of California bestowed this land to an old crony as one of his final official acts.

This grant included the San Vicente Valley, located just southeast of the present town of Ramona in San Diego County, the Barona Valley, which is north of Lakeside, and all that land in between. It involved 13,316 acres — three square leagues as measured by the Spanish and Mexicans, or 21 square miles by American standards.

The rancho is distinctive in several ways. While its rocky terrain, chaparral and oak-studded valleys combine to form a uniquely beautiful landscape, it also possesses the longest name and the most irregular boundary line of all the early California land grants.

In 2013, nearly 12,000 people resided within those boundaries. That's not many when measured by other parts of this fast growing county, but it's still considerably more than the area would have seen were it not for the vision and strong commitment of an extraordinary man.

It was not until the mid-1970s that this vast area ever held a population in excess of 300. The single event accounting for this rapid growth was the development of the planned community of San Diego Country Estates in the San Vicente Valley.

Before the Spanish soldiers and Franciscan fathers came to California in the 18th century, bands of Yuman Indians, moving west from the desert, occupied this land within well-defined village territories. The land held only as many humans as could subsist on the food that could be gathered or snared. Few reliable water springs existed, which also limited the carrying capacity of the land.

Even after the arrival of the industrious white man, who dug wells and later introduced modern well drilling equipment, the number of inhabitants remained few and far between — primarily because no early main trails crossed this land.

The usual pattern of development in Southern California has been established along roads that began as Indian trails. The Spanish explorers used these trails in their quest for treasure, and the land-hungry Anglo-Americans who followed turned them into thoroughfares.

San Vicente and Barona Valleys have always remained just off the well-traveled routes. Even today, one can enter and leave the sector only by narrow two-lane roads.

It is not certain who named San Vicente Valley in honor of Saint Vincent, or when. It is thought that Father Juan Mariner of the San Diego Mission may have been responsible. He is known to have traveled through the area during the 1790s. He referred to the valley as "un valle siempre hermosa" — the constant and beautiful valley.

14

Father Mariner explored much of what is now San Diego County to find a suitable spot for an auxiliary mission. His assignment was completed in 1796, when he recommended a river valley east of what is now Oceanside as the place for the Mission San Luis Rey. We know that Padre Barona Valley was named in honor of Father Josef Barona, who served at the San Diego Mission from 1798 until 1810. That valley was a productive part of the mission's domain, and the padre supervised the grazing of mission cattle there. He was born in Villa Nueva, Spain, in 1764 and became a Franciscan in 1783. Two years later he went to Mexico. It was during his ministry at San Diego that the mission became the largest and most prosperous in California. In 1810 he moved to Mission San Juan Capistrano where he officiated until his death in 1831.

As we drive along Wildcat Canyon Road today, we see many modern homes on the Barona Indian Reservation. Among the Indians living there, there are no doubt many descendants of those Diegueño neophytes who were baptized, married or buried by Padre Barona during his years of service here.

For the most part, the early white settlers were people merely looking for a better life. They had left the fierce winters of the East and Midwest for a gentler environment. Many came here for health reasons. They found, however, that while the weather was temperate enough, the land was basically a stubborn desert. It took only two or three winters with below normal rainfall to produce devastating results. Winter grain crops failed and herds of cattle were decimated. There has always been that critical dependence upon reliable sources of water.

The history of San Vicente Valley is highlighted by those men who attempted to improve the water supply. Efforts to exploit the groundwater potential by drilling wells, or to capture and store the vast flow of runoff that occasionally rushes through the valley, met with failure.

Early well drilling equipment was unable to penetrate the valley's thick granite floor to get to the deep aquifers that carried the higher volumes of water. Dams either silted up, washed out or had to be cut down because of disputes over water rights. Several visionaries dreamed of turning the valley into a bountiful farmland and a more populous community. But for the most part, frustration, rather than fortune, was their only reward.

It wasn't until the planned new community of San Diego Country Estates was annexed to the Metropolitan Water District, and its developer provided the necessary capital to bring water from the Ramona Municipal Water District, that San Vicente Valley's potential for good living was afforded the many, and not just the few.

Time and circumstances have been kind to the land. It is still possible to get away on a trail not far from home and hike for hours without seeing an automobile. The rancho is bordered by public lands on three sides and limited to low-residential densities. That is its main appeal to many, and that is the way it can be expected to remain.

The Early Indians

EXPLORING THE MANY OAK GROVES along San Vicente Creek, from its origin in the northeastern part of the Rancho, to its terminus at the San Vicente Reservoir, we see considerable evidence of early Indian occupation.

These first inhabitants were Yuman Indians who migrated, some two thousand years ago, from the deserts to the east to forage here for acorns.

They were two related groups, known as Tipai and Ipai, who were distinguished by their languages. Their traditional homelands were separated, approximately, by the San Diego River. The northern Ipai extended from Escondido to Lake Henshaw, and the southern Tipai included the Laguna Mountains, Ensenada and Tecate. After the Spanish Missions were established in the late 18th century, these natives were called Diegueños, since they were influenced mainly by the Mission San Diego de Alcala. They are still called by that name by many students of California Indian history.

In more modern times, however, beginning about in the 1970s and 1980s, some San Diego County tribes, notably the Viejas Band, started referring to themselves as part of

ARTIST'S CONCEPTION of an early Ipai Indian village, typical of those that were located near the San Vicente and Padre Barona Creeks. Huts were made of reeds gathered from creek beds.

the "Kumeyaay Nation." The Kumeyaay name seems to have been adopted in an effort by some Ipai speakers to reclaim their heritage and indigenous language, which characterizes ancient Tipai-Ipai culture. But the Barona Band, who are fellow Capitan Grande tribal members, have thus far chosen not to formally identify with that name. As for the U.S. Bureau of Indian Affairs, Indian tribes within the general San Diego area are officially called "Bands of Mission Indians."

Work done during the mid-1920s by amateur archaeologist John Mykrantz, who owned the upper Rancho valleys, and by anthropologists Dr. James Moriarty III and Brain Smith

INDIAN MEN on a hunting expedition. Rabbits, wood rats and quail were caught by throwing small boomerang-shaped rabbit sticks along the ground to cripple the animals.

of the University of San Diego in the 1970s, has enabled us to form a picture of the first settlers.

Evidence was found of two major villages believed to have been continuously occupied for nearly 1,800 years. One is in the area of the current southwest corner of San Vicente and Barona Mesa Roads, next to the San Vicente Golf Course, and is referred to as Iron Springs. The other is a few hundred yards southwest of the intersection of San Vicente and Wildcat Canyon Roads.

It is believed this northern valley of the San Vicente Rancho (roughly the San Diego Country Estates covenant) supported about 100 to 150 Indians, half of whom lived at each of these sites. They established this area as their territory and guarded it from intrusion by other foraging Indians. Since arable land was scare in this region's dry

BEDROCK MORTAR containing 12 grinding holes is located on the San Vicente Golf Course and represents an unusually large grinding station. Here, early day Indian women sat grinding and leaching acorns. The deeper holes were used to soak the acorns to remove their bitter tannic acid, while the shallower ones were for grinding the seeds into flour. The person pictured here is not an ancient Indian, but the author's granddaughter, Sylvan Arguello.

climate, the indigenous population had most likely reached its maximum environmental carrying capacity well before the missionaries arrived in 1769.

The Indians material culture was generally simple and involved few complex technological elements. The non-material aspects of these people's lives were, however, quite complex. Song, dance and a highly developed moral view of community behavior marked these unique people.

They were primarily gatherers and hunters, gathering acorns and wild grains and hunting small animals. The women and children collected the acorns, their main food staple. Leaving their village for a day or two at a time, they would establish stations where native oaks flourished in the creek plain, gathering acorns, and storing them to dry for several months.

These acorns were later cracked, ground in bedrock mortars and leached to remove the bitter and poisonous tannic acid. Acorn flour was later mixed with water or fat and baked into small cakes.

One such gathering and grinding station can readily be seen today adjacent to San Vicente Road, just west of and a few yards in front of the 13th tee on the golf course. It is a large granite shelf containing a dozen grinding holes (bedrock mortars). Here ancient Indian women would sit, crack, grind and leach nuts while no doubt carrying on social dialogue.

The men hunted rabbits, deer, wood rats and quail. The rodents were either snared or caught by throwing small boomerang-shaped rabbit sticks along the ground to cripple the animal. Deer were shot with bow and arrow. The rabbits were skinned and often times ground up, bones and all, and mixed with grains into a meal, which was cooked over an open fire. The skins were cured and sewn together into robes for use during cold times.

In 1926, under the auspices of the Heye Foundation's Museum of the American Indian, John Mykrantz performed an excavation of a burial ground located on a knoll near the village site toward the east end of San Vicente Road. Items found here included mortuary urns, broken grinding stones (metates), cooking pots, water jars and a ceremonial earthen pipe with a wooden stem.

Local Indians, who worked on the ranch during that time, identified this former village as Ochghwhee (spelled phonetically), a name which means, in Ipai, an onion-like tuber. The artifacts dug at this site are believed to be associated with a more recent occupation, sometime during the 17th and 18th centuries.

Other digs, of a more limited nature, conducted under the supervision of Professor Moriarty, have uncovered small arrowheads dating back 800 to 1,000 years. Also, a somewhat rare Indian pictograph of a human figure can be seen on a huge overhanging rock located behind a home on Kerri Lane. This drawing is thought to have been done by one of the early Indian shamans (medicine men).

Spanish missionaries broke up these settlements in the late 1700s. While it was far from the Franciscan missionaries intentions, the Spanish intrusion marked the beginning of the end of native Indian culture.

The land-hungry white pioneers, who followed, tended only to help drive the small Indian bands back into the more remote areas of the countryside. Those Indians who remained in the path of this wave of new settlers gradually became a source of cheap labor for the farmers and cattlemen.

The Barona Heritage

AMONG THE FIRST DIEGUEÑO NEOPHYTES brought into the newly established mission of San Diego in the 1770s were members of the Indian village of Cullamac. This rancheria (as the Spanish called such settlements) has figured in San Diego history many times. It is from this village that many of today's Barona Reservation forebearers originated. Since 1782, however, this tribal site has been known as Capitan Grande. Since 1934, it has been covered by the waters of the El Capitan Reservoir.

Don Pedro Fage, Catalin commander, and later Spanish governor of California, made several explorations between San Diego and the Colorado River during the early 1780s. An entry in his diary made on April 20, 1782, refers to his arrival at the San Diego River Canyon, calling it "el arroyo de valle de San Luis." He noted that at the junction of the San Diego River, and the mouth of the Conejos Creek, they passed the village "of the Great Captain."

How it became known as Capitan Grande is told by Hero Eugene Rensch in an article he wrote for the San Diego Historical Quarterly in July, 1956.

According to Rensch, the name comes from "Francisco el capitan de Cullamac," who was one of 15 village leaders implicated in the 1775 Indian revolt against the San Diego mission. The revolt was the outgrowth of resentment that had developed among the Indians over floggings for attending pagan dances. That, as well as the Spanish soldiers' frequent molesting of Indian women, provoked the fateful attack in which Fr. Luis Jayme became the first Franciscan martyr in New California.

As Richard F. Pourade wrote in "Time of the Bells," Fr. Jayme "couldn't believe that the Indians, whom he loved, would burn and attack a mission, or that they would kill him without thought or mercy. But they did, with uninhibited cruelty."

From that incident until now, the rancheria, as well as the area around El Capitan Reservoir, has been known as Capitan Grande, named for the rebellious Christian neophyte, Francisco, "el Capitan de Cullamac."

Cullamac is the Spanish translation of the name the Diegueño Indians gave their village. Their Indian words have subsequently been spelled at least two different ways by English speaking orthographers as "Quil-ach-nusk" and "E-quilsh-a mahk," which is Diegueño for "behind the mountain." The mountain to which they refer was known for many years as "El Capitan Mountain." Today, that 3,675-foot peak shows on the official maps as "El Cajon Mountain."

Despite whatever the early Diegueños used to call their village, those names are seldom used today, but the name Capitan Grande prevails with mapmakers and contemporary Indians, as well.

The mission period lasted nearly 60 years, from 1767 to 1833. The San Diego mission grew strong and prosperous. Baptized Indians tended large herds of cattle, cultivating and harvesting mission fields and vineyards. But also during this period, the conflict between the padres and the Spanish soldiers grew because of issues focused on morals and jurisdiction over the Indians.

The ultimate and most basic question, however, revolved around ownership of land. The Franciscans believed that California land belonged to the Indian and that the church's responsibility was to hold it in trust for them until they became civilized. The soldiers claimed otherwise — that it was the property of Spain and that private grants should provide land for soldiers, as well.

In 1821, Mexico gained independence from Spain, and with their rule came the end of Franciscan power. With secularization in 1833, the floodgate for private land grants was opened fully and the rancho era began. Those Indians who did not wander off into the backcountry, to subsist as best they could, provided cheap labor for the Dons. They received no pay in money. Heavy labor, unsanitary living conditions, bad food and raw liquor made the Indian an easy victim of the white man's diseases. The death rate among Indians was about four times that of the white man.

In 1853, a small band of Mission Indians, believed to be descendants of the pre-mission Cullamac people, requested permission to return to the land of Capitan Grande. In response, Lt. Col. John Bankhead Magruder, U.S. Army commander in San Diego, issued the following order:

Mission San Diego,
February 1st, 1853

Permission is hereby given to Patricio and Leandro, Alcalde and captain, to cultivate and live at the place called Capitan Grande, about four leagues to the south and east of Santa Ysabel, as it is with extreme difficulty that these Indians can gain a subsistence on the lands near the mission in consequence of the want of sufficient water for irrigation. It is understood that this spot, called, as above Capitan Grande, is a part of the public domain. All persons are hereby warned against disturbing or interfering with said Indians, or their people, in the occupation or cultivation of said lands. Any complaints in reference to said cultivation or to the right of occupancy must be laid before the commanding officer of the post, in the absence of the Indian agent for this part of the country.

(Signed by Lt. Col. J.B. Magruder.)

During the 1870s, settlers began moving into San Diego County in droves, and it was only a matter of time before the fertile little river valley of Cullamac was discovered by land-hungry Easterners.

In an attempt to protect the Indians' land rights, a large reservation of 19 sections was set aside for the Capitan Grande Indians in 1876. It was intended to cover some 15 miles of the San Diego River area. But as so often happened to the Indian in those days, the fertile land and village site were somehow left out of this reserve.

YELLOW SKY was a frequent visitor to the Capitan Grande village around the turn of the 20th century. He lived to be well over 100, and while often mistaken as a Capitan Grande Indian, he was not a member of that tribe. He was alleged to be an itinerant horse thief from Yuma. Ramona historian Guy Woodward heard such stories from Vic McCoy (who he knew as 'Okie Vic of Boulder Crick'). Yellow Sky supposedly stole horses in Yuma and sold them in the San Diego area; then he'd steal horses in San Diego and sell them in the Yuma area.

Their patent took in only the mountains surrounding the area. This situation naturally resulted in a dispute in 1883 between the white man and the Indian.

Helen Hunt Jackson, in her book "A Century of

Dishonor," chronicles the Indians' side through several appendixed affidavits:

> *State of California, County of San Diego:*
> *In the application of Daniel C. Isham, James*
> *Meade, Mary A. Taylor, and Charles Hensley.*

Ignacio Curo and Marcellino, being duly sworn by me through an interpreter, and the words being interpreted to each and every one of them, each for himself, deposes and says:

I am an Indian belonging to that portion of the Diegueños Indians under the captainship of Ignacio Curo, and residing in the rancheria of Capitan Grande, being also a part and portion of the Indian people known as Mission Indians; our said rancheria was located at Capitan Grande, where we all now reside in A.D. 1883, by an order issued by Colonel Magruder, of the United States Army, located at the post of San Diego on February 1st of said year, 1853. That since that time we and our families have resided on and possessed said lands. That said lands are included in township 14 south, range 2 east, of San Bernardino meridian in San Diego County, State of California.

That affiants are informed and believe that Daniel C. Isham, James Meade, Mary A. Taylor, and Charles Hensley have each of them filed in the land office of Los Angeles their application for pre-emption or homestead of lands included in the lands heretofore possessed by affiants, and now occupied by the rancheria of affiants as a home for themselves and families. That said affiants and their tribe have constantly occupied and partly cultivated the land so claimed by said Isham, Meade, Taylor, and Hensley since the year 1853. That they nor their tribe have ever signed any writing yielding possession or abandoning their rights to said lands; but that said parties heretofore mentioned are attempting by deceit, fraud, and violence to obtain said lands from affiants and the Government of the United States. Affiants therefore pray that the land officers of the United States Government will protect them in their right and stay all proceedings on the part of said claimants until the matter is thoroughly investigated and the rights of the respective parties adjudicated.

Ignacio Curo, his + mark
Marcellino, his + mark
Witness: M.A. Luce.

* * * * *

Anthony D. Ubach, being first duly sworn, on oath deposes and says: I am now, and have been continuously for the last seventeen years, Catholic pastor at San Diego, and have frequently made official visitations to the various Indian villages or rancherias in said county; that I have frequently during said time visited the Capitan Grande Rancheria, on the San Diego River, in said county of San Diego; that when I first visited said rancheria, of some seventeen years ago, the Indians belonging to the rancheria cultivated the valley below the falls on the San Diego River and herded and kept their stock as far up as said falls; that I know the place now occupied and claimed by the above-named applicants, and each of them, and also the place occupied and claimed by Dr. D. W. Strong; that from the time I first visited said rancheria until the lands were occupied, cultivated, and used by the Indians of Capitan Grande Rancheria as a part of their rancheria; that upon one occasion I acted as interpreter for Capitan Ignacio Curo in a negotiation between said Ignacio and D. W. Strong, and that said Strong at that time rented from said Ignacio a portion of the rancheria lands for bee pasturage; I also know that Capt. A. P. Knowles and A. S. Grant also rented the lands from the Indians of the rancheria when they first located there.

Anthony D. Ubach.
San Diego, State of California

At the time she wrote this book in 1886, Mrs. Jackson stated that Capitan Grande had only about 60 Indians left in the canyon, while, "Sixteen years ago there were 150 to 200 — a flourishing community with large herds of cattle and horses and good cultivated fields."

As an outgrowth of this dispute, and to the credit of the crusading Mrs. Jackson, the federal government issued a patent in 1894, firmly establishing the Indian ownership of some 15,000 acres, including Cullamac as the Capitan Grande Reservation. During the last part of the 19th century, the natives of Capitan Grande enjoyed

30

a relatively undisturbed life. A San Diego Union article of July 14, 1890, gives us a flavor of their fiesta time:

San Diego Union
July 14, 1890
Fiestas — Indian

The fiesta at Capitan Grande, the oak-shaded valley beyond Lakeside and the 'Monte' from which Rev. Father Grogen of St. Joseph's has returned, was his first experience in an Indian reservation. He says the brush chapel had been repaired, the altar end ceiled and walled with sheets, trimmed with colored prints of a sacred character, and paper flowers. Boxes covered with white curtains served for altars. He was assisted in the mass by Ignacio, the General of the tribe and the hymns of the mass were accompanied by a violin and drum.

Fifteen babies were baptized in the afternoon.

Ignacio's mother, withered, bent and toothless, said to be in her 127th year, was one of the worshipping throng. She is regarded with great veneration by the other Indians, and they were arranging to bring her to the city to sit for a photograph.

The belle of the fiesta was a miss from the Indians' school at Old Town, very neat in her shining shoes and fresh garments.

Ignacio's adobe house was the headquarters for everyone, most of the visitors camping under the big trees where each had his own fire for broiling bull steaks. A Mexican brought the animal to the valley, an Indian purchased it, cut its throat, hung its body to a tree, stripped off the hide, and afterward sold steaks for the three days of the fiesta.

Father Grogen spent the night of his stay in the chapel, rolled in blankets and had his meals served at Ignacio's where meat, eggs, vegetables and coffee were served nicely, topped off at dinner with plum pudding.

There was no other white in the settlement and he says the Indians spoke their own language altogether among themselves. When he left they were starting with their games.

The Move to Barona

WITH THE EXPLOSIVE GROWTH that came to San Diego during World War I, the city was once again searching for more reliable sources of water. The people of the Indian village of Cullamac were again thrust into the limelight when it was determined that their long river valley was a perfect place to build a dam and impound the headwaters of the San Diego River.

It took nearly 17 years, however, from the time the wheels were set in motion in 1916 until the dam actually became a reality. These were years filled with intense political and legal battling. One of the battles involved water rights, while the other was over Indian land rights.

As it developed, the Indians' interests were dealt with and settled in a relatively short time with the enactment of the "Capitan Grande Reservoir Act of 1919." This bill, which was introduced into Congress and carried by Rep. William Kettener of California, paved the way for the city of San Diego to buy the Indians' river land so the natives could purchase new reservation lands and establish new homes. Cato Sells was commissioner of U.S. Indian Affairs at the time. It was only after two years of his personal investigation, including trips to the reservation and interviews with the natives, that Sells wrote a positive report assuring favorable Congressional action.

The water rights issue lasted much longer, however, and resulted in a lengthy fight. Col. Ed Fletcher and J. A. Murray, principal owners of the Cuyamaca Water Co., claimed rights to the water flowing from the upper San Diego River. They owned the 35-mile wooden flume system that carried water from Boulder Creek to the communities of El Cajon, Lemon Grove, Spring Valley, La Mesa and East San Diego.

The City of San Diego claimed paramount rights to the entire San Diego River watershed by virtue of Spanish colonial law. Rights granted under the laws of Spain, they contended, passed successively from Spain to Mexico to California, and hence to the United States by the treaty that ended the war with Mexico.

The city fathers claimed that since it was Spain's intention to establish San Diego as a pueblo, and since the 'charter city' of San Diego was the natural successor to that intended pueblo, therefore the 20th century San Diego was the beneficiary of 18th century Spanish law entitling pueblos to all the water rights.

Col. Ed Fletcher and his colleagues from the water company didn't intend to take that one lying down.

The water rights issue was not completely settled until 1931, and only after 15 years of political maneuvering and extended lawsuits. Before the dust was finally settled,

Cuyamaca Water Co. had been awarded $600,000 for their rights. The irrigation districts of Lemon Grove, Spring Valley and La Mesa, which had been caught up in the dispute, also gained rights to a share of the storage facilities of the new reservoir.

However, about the time that all of this bickering was being sifted out, and just when the Indians began to feel the move from the Capitan Grande Reservation was at last imminent, another new wrinkle developed. The City of San Diego's hydraulic engineer, Hiram Savage, recommended that the next dam in the city's program should be built in Mission Gorge, instead of at El Capitan.

The resulting controversy consumed the better part of 1931, and the issue wasn't laid to rest until the voters of San Diego got involved. They voted to turn down the Mission Gorge idea in December 1931 and approved transfer of $3.6 million in bond money to construct a rock-filled dam at El Capitan.

Search for a New Home

Back in 1919, when legislation was adopted to compensate the Indians for their land, and when everyone realized that the Capitan Grande Indians would eventually be in the market for new reservation lands, offers of available land started rolling in.

These were unsettling years for the Indians living in Cullamac. Former Barona Tribal Chairwoman Catherine Welch recalls those years vividly. She was a small girl living on the Capitan Grande Reservation when the talk about being removed first started in 1916. She grew up

BARONA BASEBALL TEAM IN OCEANSIDE IN 1935. Pictured are (back row from left) Cay Curo, Alfred Magginni, Gene Curo and Vic Rodriguez, and in front: Bill Banegas, Martin Prieto, bat boy Frank LaChappa, John Banegas, Vincent Mesa and Paul Prieto.

and got married during that long period of uncertainty and eventually became one of the first to move to Barona in 1932.

"I remember asking my uncle (Ramon Curo Ames), when I was a little girl, 'Why don't you improve your house? Why live like this?'" Mrs. Welch told me in 1982. "And he said, 'What's the use — what's the use of improving my house? One of these days we are going to have to move out of here' — I remember that so well."

Twenty-six different parcels of land were offered to

the Office of Indian Affairs between 1922 and 1931. The land was to be owned by the Indians, but "The Great White Father," i.e., the federal government, would do the selecting and would hold these new lands in trust for the Indians.

The locations of offered parcels ranged all the way from Otay Mesa in the south to Fallbrook in the north. Six large tracts located in the Ramona-San Vicente area were among them. The 5,505-acre Barona Ranch had a price tag of $200,000 in July 1930. J. W. Mykrantz offered the 4,000-acre San Vicente Valley (now the location of San Diego Country Estates) for $192,250 in August 1930. The Vicente Ranch with its 4,300 acres — known today as Monte Vista — could have been bought for $60,000 in January 1925. In 1930, Col. Ed Fletcher, acting as agent for B.A. Etcheverry, offered that 1,000-acre Ramona ranch for $75,000, or $60,000 in cash. Other offers included the Pamo Ranch — 1,460 acres for $80,000 in 1933 — and, during that same year, F. Moretti let it be known that his 17,780-acre Santa Ysabel spread could be obtained for $400,000.

In December 1930, the City of San Diego tendered a $361,428 check to the U.S. secretary of the interior. With that, the bidding started in earnest. This was during the depth of the Great Depression and many people were losing their lands to delinquent taxes and mortgage defaults. There were few land buyers with cash and this was an opportunity not to be lost through lack of aggressiveness.

The affected Indians, however, had their own idea of what they wanted. In January 1931, a petition signed

BARONA INDIAN RESERVATION FOREMAN, Alfred Magginni, is pictured here, in about 1935.

by 64 Capitan Grande villagers was sent to the Office of Indian Affairs stating a preference for the Barona Ranch and designating Ramon Curo Ames and Bob Quitac as representatives in the matter. In March 1932, they sent yet another petition restating this choice.

ONE OF THE ORIGINAL BARONA TRIBAL LEADERS, Ramon Curo Ames, is pictured (center) at a celebration held in Lakeside in about 1949.

Barona was the place where their forebearers had worked under the direction of Fr. Barona in mission times. Many of their fathers and mothers had worked on the ranch from the late 1800s well into the 20th century — when Thomas Daley owned it in the 1880s and 1890s, when James Wadham had it at the turn of the century and when Hugh Jones Jr. farmed and grazed the land during the early part of the 1900s.

The matter had clearly boiled down to a tug-of-war between real estate agents and the Indians as to who would hold sway with the government. The validity of the signatures on the Indian petitions was questioned, and led to an investigation and report on the tribe's population and true preference. This discord served only to delay action further.

In the meantime, the Indians living in the Capitan Grande river valley village learned that the money being paid by the city for their land was also to be used to relocate the Capitan Grande Indians living in the Los Conejos village, located about three miles east of the area to be flooded. The fact that they would have to share this money with the Los Conejos band came as a surprise. But it had been determined by the government that all Indians were to be removed from the entire basin, and the money was to be allocated on an approximate $2,400 per capita share for relocation of all Capitan Grandes.

By the summer of 1932, the Barona Ranch land had finally been secured. It was purchased from the Security First National Bank of Los Angeles, which had acquired it in July 1931 in a foreclosure sale. The first group of Indians to move there comprised 12 families, thus constituting the first members of the new Barona Tribe. They moved into the Wadham and Jones ranch homes and bunkhouses, which served many of them until the promised new federal housing was finished several years later.

BIA's Grand Barona Plans

The Bureau of Indian Affairs (BIA) had not, however, been idle in planning for the relocation of these families. Much time and study was spent by the bureaucrats in designing housing and plans for creating a 'model community' on the Barona Ranch land.

Unlike some other dislocated Indian peoples in the past, the Capitan Grandes had money set aside from the sale of their land to the City of San Diego to start fresh. Irving J. Gill, a Frank Lloyd Wright trained architect and prominent San Diego building designer, was engaged to work with the Indians.

As a team, they came up with designs for one- and two-bedroom "patio" homes, complete with running water, toilets, lavatories, kitchen sinks and even built-in desks in the living rooms. (Electricity would come for these homes in 1953, when, according to tribal leader Joe Welch, his mother Catherine Welch, who was tribal chairwoman at the time, led the drive to get them hooked up with San Diego Gas and Electric Company.)

Ultimately, 16 of those homes were built by the tribe, and today, eight of these are still standing, although they are unrecognizable. Most have been remodeled over the years, and some were lost in the Cedar fire of 2003.

The Assumption of the Blessed Virgin Mary Church was also a work of Gill's, with design input and construction done by the tribe. It stands today. Other southern California tribes considered the Barona people well-off by Indian standards.

A Department of Interior census roll, dated April 1, 1933, showed that a total of 56 Indians had made the move to Barona by that time.

Los Conejos Band and Viejas

However, by October 1933, the federal government still had not finished resettling all of the Capitan Grande Indians.

Adam Castillo, president of the Mission Indian Federation, appeared on Oct. 25, 1933, before the San

Diego County Grand Jury to ask for help in speeding up the bureaucrats. "If our people are not moved," he said, "many of these peoples' homes will be under water at the first rain."

Actually, those Indians who had not been moved by then were the Los Conejos villagers who, living about three miles from the proposed reservoir site, were in little danger of ever being flooded. Apparently Mr. Castillo was stretching the point in order to get some attention.

For their new reservation, the Los Conejos villagers had chosen the beautiful Viejas Ranch, Baron Long's 1,600-acre showplace near Alpine.

As the Barona Ranch was near and familiar to the Ames-Quitac group, the Viejas Ranch was near and dear to the Conejos people. It was rich in memories for them. Many had worked there and appreciated its southern exposure and warmth in the winter.

Baron Long was a wealthy man whose extensive real estate holdings included San Diego's U.S. Grant Hotel. His Viejas horse ranch was what the Indians chose, but its asking price of $200,000 was two and a half times more than the $75,000 paid for the Barona land, which had nearly four times the acreage. Financial and political aspects combined to further delay purchase of the ranch until Long lowered his price to $150,000, which was finally negotiated down to $125,000. Unfortunately, however, even that price diminished the per capita amount of funds for each of the 78 Viejas colonists and left only enough money for cheap homes.

The federal government's foot-dragging and indecision was upsetting not only to the Indians, but to a few others, as well, as demonstrated by a handwritten, and apparently hastily scrawled, note found in the federal records. It was date-stamped as received by the Office of Indian Affairs on Oct. 28, 1933, and reads as follows:

> *John W. Collier*
> *Comm. of Indian Affairs*
> *Washington*
>
> *In re purchase of lands for Indians from fund arising from sale of El Capitan Reservation to City of San Diego, California. It appears that your department can view lands submitted by a new method = By auto travelling 35 miles per hour. view and estimate 5,600 acres in 35 minutes. This new deal and new speed method is beyond me, so I wish to withdraw my lands from further consideration. I hope that your department can keep up your speed, it is so unusual.*
>
> *By J. W. Mykrantz*
> *Ramona, California*

While some Capitan Grande Indians moved to new homes at Barona and others went to the Viejas Ranch, there was yet a third category, known as the "splinter group." They were the few who chose not to move to either of those new reservations. They took their share of the proceeds and had the government buy them land and houses in nearby communities instead.

There are no Indians living today on the vast 15,000-

HOLDING A COPY of their newly ratified constitution in 1947, Bob Quitac, Barona Tribal spokesman, explains the bylaws to his committee people: Eleanor Brown and F. T. LaChappa.

acre Capitan Grande Reservation. The tribe still does, however, own all the land that was not taken for the El Capitan Reservoir. The Barona and Viejas Bands jointly control its limited use by agreement.

The Barona population stayed nearly constant between April 1933 and 1940 when the census showed 64 residents on the reservation. About 100 acres were under cultivation with 600 acres being dry farmed in 1940.

Barona's Constitution

An unprecedented constitution was ratified by the Barona Band in 1947. Its aim was to promote tribal harmony and conserve the natural resources of their land. It still serves today as the foundation for their tribal government. Of the 31 reservations existing at that time in Southern California, the Barona Tribe was the first to institute such a wide-scale conservation program.

Robert Quitac, who was elected tribal spokesman, described the program to the San Diego Union on March 3, 1947. "The money entrusted to me and three committeemen will be used for reservation improvements and community modernization," he said. "Already we are negotiating to bring electrical power to our homes and are replacing diesel well equipment with electrically driven motors." The program was described by Quitac as a cooperative business plan to build community funds accruing from the sale of timber, crops, top soil and other resources.

Over the centuries, the Capitan Grande Indians' leader has gone by several titles, such as chief, capitan and general. Under the Barona constitution, the tribe is governed by a council with the chairperson acting as chief. Elections are conducted every four years to select these representatives. Only eight leaders (to this writing) have held the chairmanship since the formation of the Barona Band in 1932.

From 1932 to 1945, it was Ramon Curo Ames, and

MODERN-DAY TRIBAL CHIEFTAIN, Catherine Welch, who served as Barona tribal chairperson from 1948 to 1969, as photographed by the author in 1982.

from 1946 to 1947, Bob Quitac. Ames was also the Indian police force until he died in 1957.

Catherine Welch served as chairwoman from 1948 to 1969. From 1970 to 1975, it was her son Edward "Joe" Welch, and from 1976 until 1980, the chairwoman was Josephine Romero. Joe Welch served again from 1981 to 1988. From 1989 to 2004, it was Clifford LaChappa, from 2005 to 2008, Lisa Welch Scalco and from 2009 through 2012, it was Edwin "Thorpe" Romero. LaChappa was elected to serve again starting Jan. 1, 2013.

THE BARONA TRIBAL COUNCIL is the elected governing body of the reservation. Its domain encompasses 5,500 acres of land with a 2012 tribal registration of 512. The 1983 Tribal Council pictured here was (from left) Albert Phoenix, Danny Magginni, Chairman Edward "Joe" Welch, Clifford LaChappa and Daniel Curo. Since then, the council membership was expanded from five to seven. The 2013 members are Clifford LaChappa, chairman, Joe Welch, Tony Rodriguez, Adam Reyes, Beth Glasco, Bonni LaChappa and Harold Hill.

New Era on the Reservation

THE CALIFORNIA INDIANS' FASCINATION with gambling goes back to early times and their traditional game of peon. Even today, fires still burn late into fiesta and powwow nights while elders, joined by some of their younger generation, practice skills at deception, and often for high stakes. But in recent years, there's no question as to what's their favorite gambling venue.

Peon to Casinos

Today, San Diego County boasts perhaps the highest number of Indian casinos than any other county in the nation. Barona's Tribal Council oversees one of the finest gaming complexes in the West, with their first-class casino and resort.

Legalized gambling first came to their reservation in 1983 when bingo games were opened to the public. The Barona Tribe's community center, which also housed their council offices, was the place for that beginning. Expansion from bingo to a full array

INDIAN BINGO GAMING came to Barona in 1983, operating in the Community Center (pictured above), which also served as the tribe's council headquarters.

THE ORIGINAL COMMUNITY CENTER was expanded and converted into the Barona Cultural Center & Museum in 2000, and new ball fields and recreational facilities were also added.

of casino gaming evolved from there. This growth was enabled by a series of federal and state laws and referendums, which vastly advanced the California Indian gaming industry.

In 1994, the tribe, with the consulting guidance of Venture Catalyst, opened the "Barona Casino Big Top" in the center of their main valley. That business soon developed into full casino status and by 2003, those facilities had grown to embrace a 315,000-square-foot casino, a 397-room five-star resort hotel and The Barona Creek Golf Course, ranked among the top ten championship courses in California. The tribe became one of the largest employers in San Diego's East County, providing upward of 3,000 jobs.

Operations and management of this multi-million dollar business enterprise comes under the direct control of the tribal council.

One aspect of these operations involves the tribe's Gaming Commission. A branch of their government, it is responsible for regulating casino activities to comply with California gaming regulations. The four-member body is appointed by the council, and none of the four can be employed by the tribe or casino in any other aspect.

Some of us are not gamblers and don't actively promote gambling, but it's good to finally see prosperity on an Indian reservation. The Indians have certainly paid their dues, and with their new-found affluence, they have put it to constructive use for their people.

BINGO EVOLVED into casino status when new facilities were built in the reservation's central valley in the early 1990s.

BY 2003 BARONA'S CASINO and resort operations had expanded to include a 315,000-square-foot casino, a 397-room five-star hotel and the Barona Creek Golf Course.

THE NEW FACILITY housing the Barona Tribal Council and Gaming Commission, which opened in 2010, received a national award for its environmentally friendly design and construction.

Member Services

Tribal population, or enrollment, as it's called, numbered 512 as of December 2012. Direct lineage and one-eighth blood quantum determine eligibility for tribal membership.

The Tribal Council provides their people with extensive programs and services. In many ways, their government organization mirrors that of an efficient municipality. It has a full-time fire department with the latest equipment and facilities. Their tribal enforcement department is a fully staffed operation, protecting their community, as well as visitors.

The Barona Tribe provides 100 percent medical, dental and vision insurance coverage for all tribal members, their nonmember spouses, children and dependents.

The reservation's wastewater treatment facility that services the extensive gaming and resort operations is

BARONA'S TRIBAL SEAL features the Assumption of the Blessed Virgin Mary Church to honor the tribe's heritage.

state of the art, and reclaimed water is used for irrigating the golf course and for landscaping.

Housing and Cultural Advancements

Opportunities for home ownership by tribal members is encouraged and supported. A member may choose a home site in various areas of the reservation's 5,500 acres where there are developed roads and available electric service. Construction financing is available through the council with no-interest loans. In order for a tribal member to qualify, he/she must be over 18 years of age and possess a high school diploma or equivalent. To date, more than 85 new homes have been financed through that program.

There is also a Senior Home Improvement program

that fully funds the rehabilitation of their elders' homes to modern and improved standards.

Most members of the Barona tribe work away from the reservation in neighboring communities. The tribe most closely associates itself with the Lakeside community since this is where their post office has been ever since they lived in Capitan Grande and where their children have gone to school.

Today's children, K thru 12, still attend schools in Lakeside in the Sweetwater Unified School District. There's also a public charter school on the reservation, which was established by the tribe for grades K–8, with a fully accredited faculty and latest technology.

Financial assistance for education is offered by the tribe, with full college scholarships awarded to members' children who qualify academically.

The Barona Cultural Center & Museum was built in January 2000 and stands where their original community center once was. It is dedicated to the perpetuation and presentation of native culture, and is open to the public.

The Rancho's First Church

One of the first improvements made by the Barona Indians after acquiring their reservation land was the establishment of a church. The original church still stands prominently today on Wildcat Canyon Road across from the main entrance to the resort.

Barona Indians are, for the most part, Roman Catholic, as are other Mission Indians of this region. This first church to be built within the old Rancho

FATHER MICHAEL X. TRAM is the current pastor for the Saint Kateri Tekakwitha National Indian Mission parish.

BROTHER EDWARD NOLAN (left), who came to Barona in 1978 is the current Pastoral Coordinator for the parish. He is shown in 1982 with Father Alan P. Beauregard, who was tribal pastor at the time.

San Vicente boundaries is named the Assumption of the Blessed Virgin Mary, and was dedicated on Aug. 14, 1934. Its classic mission design was the work of a noted San Diego architect, Irving J. Gill, and stands in recognition of early Barona settlers and their descendants.

Father Michael X. Tram is the current pastor for the Saint Kateri Tekakwitha National Indian Mission parish. The parish includes Barona and two other reservations, Viejas and Sycuan, and is part of the San Diego Catholic Diocese. The parish is named in honor of a 17th century Algonquin-Mohawk Indian maiden who was sainted for her work with the poor and for various miracles.

Brother Edward Nolan, who is Pastoral Coordinator for the three reservations, came to Barona in 1978 and has been close to their people since.

Commercial Enterprise

Barona Tribal business affairs have become more diversified since their constitution was first adopted. Besides their casino and resort operations, the tribe leases land to organized groups who sponsor auto drag racing and motorcycle racing. However, the open-range grazing of cattle is no longer prevalent because of the increased impact of traffic on Wildcat Canyon Road.

The people of Barona customarily celebrate their annual powwow over Labor Day weekend. Open to the public, the Barona PowWow attracts Indians from reservations throughout the West. Contests are held for drummers and for dancers, who are usually dressed

ULTRALIGHT AIRCRAFT pilots were frequently seen above the valleys, until the Cedar Fire of 2003 destroyed the facility.

MOTOCROSS ENTHUSIASTS have found a home on the Barona Indian Reservation.

BARONA SPEEDWAY is San Diego's only semi-banked quarter-mile clay oval track. It features a wide variety of cars including Pro Stocks, Pony Stocks, Factory Stocks, Pure Stocks, Modifieds, Dwarf Cars and Mini Dwarfs.

in elaborate and beautifully colored Indian attire. And the Barona men challenge those of other bands at their favorite games of peon and softball. This event is an opportunity for everyone to enjoy good beef barbeque and get better acquainted with their Indian friends and neighbors. Proceeds from concession stands and barbecue dinners go to support the tribe's recreation programs and church.

VISITING INDIANS FROM ARIZONA perform at the 1982 annual Barona Reservation Labor Day PowWow (above), while Barona tribal members sing and dance under the oaks (below).

San Vicente's First Don

IN 1846, DURING THE WANING DAYS of Mexico's rule in California, the last Mexican governor, Pio Pico, generously conferred land grants to his many friends, colleagues and political allies. One of those grants was the "Rancho Cañada de San Vicente y Mesa del Padre Barona." It is one of the longest titles applied to a Mexican rancho, and, translated into English, means "the glen of St. Vincent and the plateau of Father Josef Barona." That grant went to one of Pico's sidekicks of the 1831 revolution against Governor Victoria.

We know very little about the first nonaboriginal landlord of San Vicente. What we do know of him has been pieced together from many sources. He was baptized Juan Bautista Lopez at the Mission San Miguel, Baja California, in 1786. He migrated to the San Gabriel area, and in 1808 he was married at the Mission San Gabriel to Maria Josefa Verdugo. She was the daughter of Jose Maria Verdugo, owner of the 36,403-acre Rancho San Rafael, which covered what is now Glendale and Burbank.

Verdugo, a "soldado de cuera" (leather jacket soldier), accompanied Capt. Fernando Rivera to Alta California and was only the second to receive a Spanish land grant in this area. The first was Juan Jose Dominguez, who was granted the 43,119 acres that now cover all of the southern part of Los Angeles County. With such extensive land holdings, the descendants of these retired soldiers, called "invalidos," had little difficulty in attaining racial, social and political status in Mexican California.

Juan and Maria later moved to San Diego. We have no clue as to when they moved, or what Juan's main occupation was. H. H. Bancroft writes, in his "History of California," that during the revolt of 1831, "when the pronunciamento was being prepared in San Diego, Pio Pico and Juan Lopez made visits to Los Angeles to enlist the Angelinos."

Juan's two brothers, Ignacio and Bonifacio, were prominent in San Diego affairs. Ignacio had been a "leather jacket soldier" at the San Diego presidio and corporal in charge of his escort. He was later elected to the Mexican California legislature in 1822 and took part in the revolt of 1831 with Juan.

Under the Ayuntamiento de 1835, that established the San Diego municipal council, Juan's brother Bonifacio was designated "Judge of the Plains." As such, it was his responsibility to oversee the rodeos and matanzas (butchering of cattle), and settle disputes over the ownership of cattle grazing in the hills and valleys that were being broken away from mission control. Bonifacio was popularly known as "The King," and his corral in Old Town was known as "el corral del rey."

A SILVER DON of the 1850s, Andres Pico, brother of Pio Pico and leader of the victorious Californios in the Battle of San Pasqual, is shown here in the dress of the more affluent Dons of the period. Unlike Pico, Don Juan Lopez had little more to show as his wealth than the land granted him.

In 1834, Juan Lopez petitioned the governor for the Rancho Secuan in the general area of what is now known as Dehesa. The expediente requested two leagues of land (approximately 8,900 acres) "bounded by the Rancho Jamacha and the Mission of San Diego."

Juan Osuna, in a report to Governor Alvarado, stated that Lopez has five children and "possesses some means, however but little, but is a man of industrious habits which the committee believes will advance his interests." Alvarado issued the grant for Secuan to Lopez on May 2, 1839. Records do not show how long the Lopezes lived on that ranch. There is no diseño (map) of the property in the archives since that rancho was never claimed before the U.S. Land Commission.

Why the Lopezes left Secuan is not known. It could have been that the drought of 1841 and the lack of a reliable water source drove him to seek better land. It could have been the intense Indian hostility that prevailed then in that area, or both. Whatever the reason, we know that he moved to the San Vicente Valley about 1843.

On Sept. 1, 1845, Lopez filed an expediente with Governor Pio Pico stating, "I ask for the place known as Cañada of San Vicente as far as the mesa called Padre Barona." On Jan. 25, 1846, the grant was conferred.

In 1848, with the United States' victory over the Mexicans, California became a U.S. territory. The treaty of Guadalupe Hidalgo guaranteed that legitimate California land titles would be respected. The U.S. Land Commission was formed in 1851 to examine all ranch claims and determine legal ownership of land granted to private citizens.

In 1852, Domingo Yorba, the man who acquired the rancho from Lopez, filed a petition with the commission for confirmation of title to the rancho. From commission records of this land case, we gain

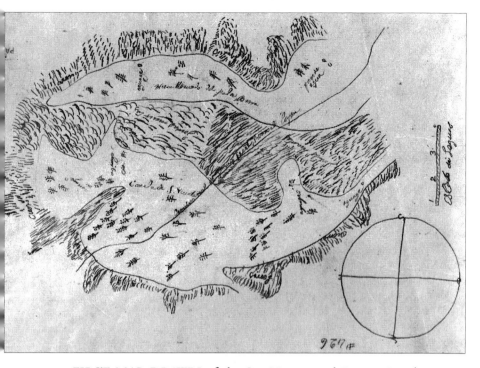

FIRST MAP DRAWN of the San Vicente and Barona Rancho. This diseño was drawn and presented to the U.S. Land Commission in 1852 as part of the claim of Domingo Yorba for the grant land. It is interesting to compare this map with the boundary established by the U.S. Surveyor General in 1869 (see Rancho Map page xi). Note: This diseño faces south.

some insight into the Lopezes' life at San Vicente during the years of 1843-1847.

Three witnesses appeared on behalf of the claimant. They were Jose Antonio Elizalde, J. J. Warner and Abel Stearns. Stearns testified as to the authenticity of the signatures of Governor Pico, Jose R. Arguello, and other officials involved in the 1846 grant. Elizalde, age 32, testified on Nov. 10, 1852:

"He (Lopez) had a house, a corral and a garden. He lived in the house with his family. He had a small stand of corn and tame horses and cultivated part of the ground. Lopez left the place on account of the war and of trouble from the Indians. The land is in the frontier in the mountains. When the Americans came, Leonardo Cota, who had the command of the Californios, warned the inhabitants to abandon their ranch and drive their cattle from the border (?) into the interior."

(Note: Commission records were in longhand and some words are hard to decipher.)

It is difficult to place the exact location of the Lopez home from the diseño (map) filed with the Land Commission in 1852. However, the first official survey of the rancho, made in 1869 by the U.S. Surveyor General, depicts the ruins of Lopez's adobe house in the general area of what is now the east end of San Vicente Golf Course, near Indian Head Court.

By 1846, Juan Lopez was a man of 60. Contrary to popular belief, the life of a typical Don in San Diego during the 1840s was no life of luxury. Some writers have depicted these old rancho days as one long fiesta, with the Dons riding majestic horses with silver saddles, and the beautiful senoras not having a care in the world. But Don Juan's rancho was far from opulent. The hacienda had two or three rooms at most, with a dirt floor and a cowhide for a door. There was no comfortable furniture and only the barest necessities.

THE LOPEZ RANCHO HOUSE as it is believed to have appeared in 1844-1846 when Don Juan Lopez and family lived in the San Vicente Valley. The site of the ranch house was located just off the east end of the present-day Indian Head Court.

With the Indians an almost constant threat, and the war with the Americans causing further uncertainty, Juan and Maria moved back to Old Town San Diego to be near friends and relatives. They had tried to hack out a living at San Vicente for about three years, but life on the frontier was too harsh, especially for those in their sunset years.

A map of Old Town in 1850, made by Cave J. Couts, shows the house of Juan Lopez situated next to that of Santiago Arguello, his friend of many years. We don't know where or when Don Juan died, but the San Diego Mission records indicate that Doña Maria Josepha Verdugo Lopez lived out her remaining years in San Diego. She was buried at Campo Santos in 1863.

Don Domingo

ON MAY 13, 1850, Juan Lopez deeded the Rancho San Vicente to Domingo Yorba. California was about to be admitted as a state and the County of San Diego became the new state's first county. By this time, Don Juan was 64. Coping with these changes would have been hard enough for a younger man, but for Lopez, it must have been difficult. With the formation of the county under the Act of February 18, 1850, came the inevitable property tax. Living in Old Town, Lopez could not have been receiving much income from his rancho, yet the county and state were looking to him for help in supporting their new government.

The first tax roll of 1850 for the County of San Diego (which was saved from the incinerator by the San Diego Historical Society in a Court House cleaning in 1937) shows the Lopez rancho with a total assessment of $4,819. For every hundred dollars of assessed value in 1850, San Diegans paid 50 cents to the state, 25 cents to the county, and 25 cents for a new county court house. They also paid $8 in poll taxes. These new taxes meant that

LIST OF PROPERTY, REAL AND PERSONAL, OF _Domingo Vesa_
Subject to Taxation in the County of San Diego, State of California.

NAME OF RANCH.	NO. LEAG'S	NO. ACRES.	TOWNSHIP	VALUE	VAL. IMP'TS
San Vicente	8	7331/6		$1000	$100.00
					$1100.00

PERSONAL PROPERTY.

CLASS.	NUMBER.	VALUE.	CLASS.	NUMBER.	VALUE.
Wild Cattle,	300	$2,100.00	Goods,		
Gentle Cattle,			Money,		
Oxen,			Mortgages,		
Wild Horses,	40	$320.00	Vessels,		
Gentle Horses,	10	250.00	Notes,		
Wild Mules,			Bonds,		
Gentle Mules,			Scrip,		
Goats,			Assn,		
Sheep,			Other Personal Property.		$50.00
Hogs,		$2,670.00	Total Amount		$2720.00

CITY LOTS: AS DESIGNATED UPON THE OFFICIAL MAP.

NO. LOT.	NO. BLOCK.	SIZE.	VALUE IMP'MTS.	NO LOT.	NO. BLOCK.	SIZE.	VALUE

at Ranch were
found no one there
to give in Property
the above was left with
Jose Ma Estudillo by
the man in charge to
give to me

I do solemnly swear that the above is a true and correct list of all my personal and real property, subject to taxation within the County of San Diego.
Sworn and subscribed to before me,
this 23d day of
186/

James McCoy County Assessor.

Don Juan now owed the government the handsome sum of $490 for the honor of being an absentee landlord. This tax bill would undoubtedly be only the first of many more to come. We don't know if this new taxation was the main reason he let the rancho go, but it obviously played a major role in the decision. There also had to be some apprehension in Don Juan's mind about perfecting title to his land under the rules of the new government.

The man who acquired the land from Lopez was Domingo Yorba, a member of the prominent Yorba family who owned most of what is now Orange County. H. H. Bancroft, in his "History of California," incorrectly identifies him as Jose Domingo Yorba, born in 1795, son of Jose Antonio Yorba I. Actually, the Domingo who became the new don of San Vicente was Domingo de la Resurrección Yorba, born in 1826. Jose Domingo, who in actuality did not live to be 2 years of age, was the new owner's deceased uncle.

The Yorba dynasty started with Jose Antonio Yorba I who, as a youthful soldier, had served under Portola in

PROPERTY TAX DECLARATION DATED 1861 for all San Vicente property subject to San Diego County taxes (shown left). Domingo Yorba placed a value of $1,000 for tax purposes on the 13,316 acres contained in the rancho. The ranch house was valued at $100, his 300 head of cattle at $2,100, 40 wild horses at $320 and 10 gentle horses at $250. The note in the lower right-hand corner was made by the assessor. It states, "At Ranch twice found no one there to give in property the above was left with Jose Ma. Estudella by the man in charge to give me." Estudello was a Wells Fargo agent at the time and the Wells Fargo office in Old Town served as the place to leave messages and notices.

1769. He married the daughter of Capitan Pablo Grijalva, and after retiring as a "sargento invalido," went into business with his father-in-law, grazing cattle on the Santa Ana River. In 1810 he received a Spanish land grant for the Rancho Santiago de Santa Ana. Thus began the Yorba domain in Orange County.

Domingo's father, Jose Antonio II, was politically inclined. He served as "alcalde" (mayor) at Santa Ana Abajo in 1830, and "juez de paz" (justice of the peace) in 1840. In 1847 he was a "regidor" (councilman) of the Los Angeles legislative council with a jurisdiction over all of present-day Orange County. Domingo's uncle Bernardo was famous as the first recognized large-scale farmer in California.

Jose Antonio II died when Domingo was 23 years old, leaving him the family adobe, "El Refugio," and a share of the Rancho Santa Ana. Domingo married Maria Rios, and they eventually had eight children. In 1854, he sold his inherited property to purchase the Rancho Niguel, known today as Laguna Niguel, where he lived during the time he owned Rancho San Vicente.

Domingo acquired San Vicente when he was but 24 years old. The fact that a man so young would be involved in such a large sale, along with the highly unusual terms of the sale, would lead one to believe that some strong family ties must have influenced the deal. Indeed, this apparently was the case because Domingo's mother, Maria Catalina, was a Verdugo and she and Don Juan Lopez's wife were sisters.

Lopez deeded San Vicente, including 32 head of cattle, to Domingo Yorba in return for a bond for $2,000. The bond guaranteed that Domingo would "properly clothe and maintain the said Juan Bautista Lopez and Maria Josepha Verdugo, his wife, during each of their material lives." The few published accounts regarding this transaction make a point of the fact that the Mexican, Lopez, signed the deed with an 'X.' They fail to note that the Spaniard, Yorba, signed the bond with an 'X,' as well. He, too, was illiterate.

For nearly 20 years, the cattle grazing on Rancho San Vicente bore the Yorba brand. The Yorba adobe was located about a mile west of the old Lopez home. It was just across San Vicente Creek, southwest of what is now number five green on the San Vicente Golf Course.

County tax statements give some clues to the operation of the ranch from the first Yorba statement found, dated May 31, 1856, to the last one of March 11, 1869. They estimate the land's worth, who was in charge, and how many horses and cattle were being run each year.

In 1856, Yorba claimed the rancho contained "dos" (two) leagues rather than "tres" (three), and that it was worth $1,500. His 200 head of cattle were valued at $1,000 ($5 each) and his 30 "bestias caballares" (riding horses) were worth $10 each. Valuation, land and personal property totaled $2,800. Property taxes by then had increased 50 percent over those that Lopez faced in 1850, yet Yorba was liable for only $428 in 1856.

From about 1859 until about 1863, Yorba, the absentee owner, had a majordomo by the name of Ysidro Silbas running the ranch and signing the tax statements in his behalf. The most cattle run on the ranch while Yorba owned it was 535 head in 1862 — 500 belonging to

Yorba and 35 to Silbas. Prices were depressed that year (at least for tax purposes), as the value per head was placed at $4. Just three years earlier, they were worth $8 each.

From 1863 until about 1866, Yorba had a man by the name of Librado Silvas running the operation. It is most probable that, in spite of the difference in spelling ('b' and 'v') of the two last names, the two men were related. Ysidro signed his own name to the statements while Librado made a mark. The assessor wrote in the name with a "v," which in all likelihood should have been a "b," as the Spanish "v" sounds similar to "b."

In any event, the Silbases were gone by 1867 and the tax statements from that year through 1869 were "sworn to and subscribed to" the county assessor by Yorba himself with his own mark.

During those last years of Yorba ownership, the number of cattle diminished from 250 head in 1866 to but 70 in 1869. At no time during the period he owned the rancho did Yorba value the 13,316 acres at more than $1,664.25, at least so far as the tax collector was concerned.

San Vicente was not the only rancho in the San Diego area where the Yorba brand was found during that era. Domingo's nephew, Jose de Garcia Yorba, grazed cattle on the National Ranch in the early 1860s while his cousin Raimundo and uncle Bernardo ran cattle at San Luis Rey during the mid-1860s. The Yorbas were a most industrious family indeed, and their interests were spread all over Southern California.

One of Domingo's first orders of business, shortly after acquiring the Rancho San Vicente in 1850, was to

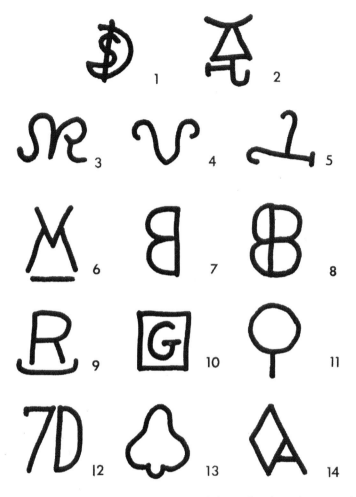

CATTLE BRANDS: Here are some of those that have been used on the San Vicente and Barona Rancho over the years.

1. Mission San Diego de Alcala
2. Domingo Yorba
3. Mykrantz/Scarbery
4. Banegas
5. Quitac
6. Hawn/Summers
7. Barnett
8. Bassett
9. Romero
10. Humiston
11. Magginni
12. Dukes
13. Banegas
14. Phoenix

make sure his title was secure under the laws of the new government of the United States.

The Land Act of 1851, creating the U.S. Land Commission, required that all land claims be submitted within two years, or the land owner would forfeit his rights. The burden of proof was placed on the Dons, but the majority of those land-rich Californios were money poor.

Lengthy legal procedures, as well as the fact that the hearings were conducted in San Francisco, proved costly for the southern claimants. Witnesses, who were in most cases close friends, had to be transported and lawyers had to be hired. Lawyers' fees for presenting a claim ran from $50 for small tracts to $1,700 for large grants. Some rancheros had to borrow money at exorbitant rates to fight for their claim. Some were hard-pressed to locate carelessly drawn titles and maps.

In the case of Don Domingo, he presented his claim, and his case was heard in November of 1852, with further testimony taken in October 1853. The Commission confirmed the grant on Dec. 2, 1854. The official patent, however, was nearly some 20 years in coming. By 1859, the U.S. Land Office had not issued a single southern patent. These patents required a survey by the U.S. Surveyor General and, apparently, San Diego was at the wrong end of the state. The Rancho San Vicente survey was finally conducted in the fall of 1869 by Deputy U.S. Surveyor Vitus Wackenreuder, a name familiar to anyone who has read the legal description of his San Vicente property.

The 1852 Yorba claim was accompanied by a crudely

drawn "diseño." It is difficult to see much similarity between what that map depicts and the 1869 U.S. survey. The Mexican and Spanish methods of establishing boundaries were loose, at best. The phrase "poco mas o menos" (a little more or less) was used to cover errors in estimates. In the case of claims before the U.S. Land Commission, testimony from a reliable person was often needed to reinforce the boundary claim. Such testimony was forthcoming on Yorba's behalf from J.J. Warner, who in 1844 was granted the Rancho San Jose del Valle, known today as Warner's Ranch.

On Oct. 21, 1853, Warner, then a state senator, testified:

"I am acquainted with the said tract. I first knew it in 1844 or 1845. It was then occupied by Juan Lopez who continued to occupy it down to the time of the insurrection in the winter of 1846 and 1847.

"He had a dwelling house upon it. It was occupied by himself and family. He had some small fields under cultivation and a kitchen garden.

"It is situated in the County of San Diego about twenty miles northeast of the mission of San Diego. It consists of two valleys. The Valleys are highly elevated above the ocean surrounded by a high and well defined mountain absolutely disconnected from any other arable or grazing land.

"The water courses leading from it running through impassable gorges. The surrounding mountains are barren, very rocky and mostly are destitute of forest trees."

(Commission question) "What do you think the area included in these two valleys?"

"I should think not to exceed two and a half or three leagues. I have practiced surveying on a small scale in California and have some experience. I should further state that this tract of land is well understood in San Diego County and the boundaries by which it is defined are well known."

About four years after the U.S. survey was completed, and 21 years after Yorba filed his claim, the patent was finally issued. On Nov. 17, 1873, by order of President U. S. Grant, the boundary was certified by the Commissioner of the General Land Office, Willis Drummond. Don Domingo had sold the rancho five years earlier.

Early Speculators

EARLY IN 1864, the San Diego County Board of Supervisors ordered a road survey through the Rancho San Vicente land grant. It was only the 12th such survey to be made by the fledgling county and shows on the records today as O.S. (Old Survey) 12. The route followed the well-worn mission and Indian trail leading out of the El Cajon Valley through Lakeside to the Padre Barona Creek. From the Barona Valley it wound north to the San Vicente Valley, taking a course somewhat close to that of Wildcat Canyon Road today.

Before reaching San Vicente Valley, according to survey notes, it "ran southwest along the base of a high conical hill," then dropped down into the valley to join, at the Yorba ranch adobe, the trail from Santa Maria Valley. The route continued up the valley to leave through the north saddle and join the trail to Santa Ysabel. On July 5, 1864, the supervisors called for proposals to build a road along this alignment, but none were forthcoming. The route was to remain but a rough trail for several years more.

The rancho remained off the beaten path. Domingo Yorba continued to graze cattle, and the tax assessor continued to make his predictable annual spring trek to the valley to count cattle. Other than that, nothing much was happening.

By 1868, due primarily to Alonzo Horton's promotional activities, San Diego started to experience a land boom. The Kimball brothers bought the "Rancho de La Nacion," and so began the development of National City. The going price for good open land in San Diego County was now up to more than $1 per acre.

After 18 years of ownership, Yorba must have thought the time was right to sell Rancho San Vicente. On Nov. 5, 1868, he conveyed title to Charles V. Howard for a total consideration of "Eight Thousand Dollars, Gold Coin of the United States of America." On that same day, Howard conveyed one-half undivided interest in the property to Prudent Beaudry, J. G. Downey and G. A. Hayward for the total sum of "Eight Thousand Dollars, lawful money of the United States of America." Whatever the understanding, the obvious outcome of that transaction was that Howard came out of the deal with half the ranch at no cost to himself.

This, it seems, was the second of two San Diego speculative land deals in which Howard, Beaudry and Downey were partners. One month earlier, the three had purchased 62 San Diego city lots for the total price of $5,000. We don't know how they faired on that venture. We do know they were able to sell the Rancho San Vicente less than one year later for $20,000, a most lucrative 150 percent return on investment for

Beaudry, Downey and Hayward — and an even niftier profit for Howard.

One of those four partners, John G. Downey, was a man well known around the state of California. He had become governor in 1860, less than 15 years after arriving in the state with but $10 in his pocket. He was a native of Ireland, with a distinguished ancestry. In 1850 Downey opened a drugstore in Los Angeles, and it was the only one between San Diego and San Francisco. Within three years he had accumulated $30,000 and was on his way to amassing a large fortune from land deals and cattle raising. He purchased 75,000 acres where the cities of Downey and Wilmington and the Port of San Pedro now stand. But he must have also had a liking for the San Diego area, because some years later, he also bought the Warner's Ranch.

In May 1869, the Central and Union Pacific Railroads met at Promontory Point, Utah, marking the beginning of real growth for the young state of California.

In October 1869 the Downey group was able to sell the rancho to a syndicate made up of some 19 different people, most of whom lived in San Francisco. Ownership was distributed among the new owners in undivided interests. Apparently there was a plan for each to receive definite parcels once the U.S. government survey was completed. That survey was finished in December and the actual partitioning of land to individuals began in March 1870.

Judge Charles H. Chamberlain of San Francisco was appointed trustee. Parcels were distributed in a rather odd fashion, leading one to believe the assignments were made by lot, at least in part. For example, John Rutman was granted his 599-acre share of land in two parcels, one in the extreme east end of San Vicente Valley, and the other in the middle of the valley — three miles apart.

Several others found their holdings situated similarly. This method of distribution later complicated things for those intending to pursue serious productive use of the land. When Augustus Barnett, James Dukes and James Stockton acquired valley land in the 1880s, they had to work out land swaps in order to assemble logical working ranches.

It appears that, for the most part, this San Francisco group bought purely for speculation. There were three of them, however, who did actually move to their properties and take up residency.

One was B. S. Sargeant, who settled on about 200 acres in the Long's Gulch area of the upper Barona and lived there for 13 years. On May 4, 1881, the San Diego Union reported that Sargeant "had prospects for a very good honey crop." His main interest, it said, was cattle, but he also "was raising horses and had put a few acres in grain for hay." In 1883 Sargeant sold his holdings, which had grown to 700 acres, to John B. Rea of El Cajon, and moved to the Arizona territory.

Edward C. Havener acquired an undivided 320 acres in November 1869 and was the first to settle in the Ramona Oaks area of the San Vicente Valley. It is said Havener was a retired Navy man.

One of those San Francisco investors managed to have a prominent landform named after himself within

SPANGLER PEAK, as viewed looking west down San Vicente Road.

a month of becoming a part owner in the rancho. It seems D. B. Spangler came down on the coastal steamer, "Senator," in November 1869 to take a look at what he'd just bought into. He must have crossed paths with the crew who was in the process of doing the boundary survey. No telling what he told them, or paid them, but the peak bordering San Vicente Road, just across from the ruins of the old dam, shows on the original survey of December 1869 as "Mtn. Spangler." That name remains on official government maps to this day, a tribute to one of San Vicente Valley's earliest land speculators.

Another prominent landmark was named during

that same survey. Gower Mountain, bordering the northeast boundary, is named for George Gower, a surveyor and member of that first survey crew. A few months later, as it developed, he struck it big with two other men in the discovery of the Washington gold mine in Julian on Washington 's Birthday in 1870.

While government maps have since referred to it only as Gower Mountain, early settlers, going back to the turn of the century, knew it by two other names. According to Sam Quincey, great-grandson of James Stockton, it was called "Slingshot," the name apparently given to the shape of the structure. Later, however, people began calling it "Black Horse" mesa or mountain.

"The new name came about," according to a story his mother Edna Stockton Quincey told him, "due to a black mare that ran away from the Warnocks in Ballena. The mare was chased down, but lost, last seen close to the mountain. Though never seen again, apparently she produced a male colt that when mature suddenly appeared up on the mesa top. The stallion looked for all the world like his black mother. He lived on top, taking advantage of a spring, but ranged quite a distance. This was appreciated by the ranchers that lost mares to his harem. Apparently the wild spirit and independence of the black stallion appealed to the settlers as they chose to permit him his freedom (as well as his mares). Sam, Bob and Jim Warnock used to spin a tale about the black mare and her stallion offspring."

Another version of how Black Horse Mountain got its name came from Mary Dukes Walters. "Well, this is as my mother tells it," she said. "There were some

GOWER MOUNTAIN, otherwise known as Black Horse Mesa, is shown here in 1974, shortly after the opening of the San Vicente Golf Course.

miners that were looking for the lost Peg Leg Mine, and they got up in the hills, and they had a little black colt with them. When they left, I don't know just how the little black colt stayed behind, but they lost it. So they left anyway, and they left that little black colt to roam those hills. So he did. He roamed those hills until he got to be a great big beautiful black stallion. Well, there were different ones would try to catch him and they never could catch him. He'd just outwit 'em. So finally they did. They got up there and they run him out of the hills, and they run him clear down through San Vicente Valley, clear down to Santa Maria Valley, and they run him so hard, he died. That's the story."

Two versions. One from a descendant of the Dukes and another from the Stocktons. Take your pick.

The 1870s

THE DECADE OF THE 1870s didn't prove to be the most opportune for backcountry land speculators. It was marked by a general slowdown in the San Diego economy in 1873, and in 1875, by a statewide depression in which the Bank of California failed.

In April 1870, the County Board of Supervisors, deciding to do something about the physical condition of the road through the Barona area, declared O.S. (Old Survey) 12 a "public highway," and put their money where their mouths were by appropriating $250 to improve it. By 1874, that "public highway" needed some repairs and the supervisors appropriated another $150. B. S. Sargeant was appointed overseer of that work.

Despite the slow times, the San Francisco syndicate was actively seeking out prospective customers for their San Vicente holdings. The Nov. 18, 1873 edition of the San Diego Union carried the following advertisement:

```
┌──────── RANCH FOR LEASE ────────┐
│  3,000 acres of the best part of the main  │
│  valley of the San Vicente Rancho lying    │
│  between the Cajon and the Santa Maria. Or │
│  will sell to a colony of a dozen families on │
│  most favorable terms or will exchange for │
│  town property.                             │
│     Title from United States perfected.     │
│     Apply at San Vicente Ranch for a short  │
│  time, or to McDonald & Co., San Diego.     │
└─────────────────────────────────┘
```

Gold fever hit the backcountry after the big discovery in Julian. However, instead of solid families moving into the valleys as envisioned, most of the inhabitants were gold-panning squatters during the first part of that decade.

One young man, destined to play a big role in San Diego County affairs over the next 40 years, appeared on the scene about this time. For a brief period in the history of the rancho, he would frequently gallop the full length of the grant land, through rugged gulches and over steep grades. Chester Gunn, while in his early 20s, established a pony express mail service between San Diego and Julian in 1871.

It was just hard work, with little romance. Julian had grown up overnight, as most gold camps did, and was only reached by long and rough roads over which supplies had to be shipped by wagon. Mail delivery was catch-as-catch-can, and received only when some wholly trustworthy person was going that way. There were no stage lines and no way to reach the backcountry except to buy or hire a rig to make the two-day journey.

In a 1924 interview with the San Diego Union, Mr.

Gunn, recalling those days, said, "It seemed to me that there ought to be good money in fast service. I was out of a job just then, so I started this pony express on my own responsibility. I charged ten cents a letter and carried letters and small packages. The people up there were glad to pay that much for they knew they'd get their mail as soon as it came in, instead of having to wait until someone happened to be going up.

"In those days San Diego got its mail by ship. A ship came in once a week. For a long time it had been only once a month, but as the town grew, it was increased to a ship every two weeks, and later to a ship a week. I only made one trip a week to Julian, but I made the trip in good time and regularly, and the people depended on me.

"The wagon road to Julian was a different route from the one traveled today. It went up over Poway to the San Pasqual Valley, then over into the Ramona Valley. Ramona was the first night's stop. Then the road went up through Santa Ysabel and then up to Julian. It was about 80 miles long. I never could have made my trip up one day and down the next if I had followed that route. So I followed the Indian trails up into the Cajon Valley, then up San Vicente to Ramona and through Santa Ysabel to Julian.

"It was a hard trip. I started the service in the fall and kept it up all through the winter, about six months. I had to make the trip in all kinds of weather, wet and sloppy, muddy, slippery trails, and cold winds with sleet and snow.

"Then Joe Foster, who's supervisor now, and a man named Frary, started a stage line. The stage made the trip in one day, so there was no use for my pony express."

Gunn went on to become Julian's Wells Fargo agent, and

CHESTER GUNN, a pony express rider as a young man, later became Julian's Wells Fargo Agent and U.S. Postmaster and a distinguished San Diego County Supervisor. He's pictured here in 1923, more than 50 years after he rode the mail the full length of the grant land on a weekly basis.

later that year, the first postmaster of the town's new post office. He was active in mining and is said to have planted the first apple orchards in that area. In 1889, Governor Robert Waterman appointed him to an unexpired term on the County Board of Supervisors and he was later elected, in his own right, to one term.

Gunn served on the commission that split off parts of San Diego County to form the new counties of Riverside in 1893 and Imperial in 1907. He was the cousin of Douglas Gunn, one of the founders of the San Diego Union and later mayor of the City of San Diego.

Gunn Stage Road, the main thoroughfare from San Vicente Road to the northern part of the valley, was named in honor of Chester. The developers of San Diego Country Estates admittedly took some liberty in the naming of that road. It was felt that a name such as "Gunn Pony Express Road" would be too long and awkward, and settled instead for the present name.

Gold, Copper & Buried Treasure

GOLD WAS DISCOVERED in Julian in early 1870 and the fever it generated resulted in considerable prospecting activity in the Rancho San Vicente area.

But it wasn't just the lure of that precious mineral that caught the interest of fortune hunters to these parts. Where thar's gold there often are profitable deposits of copper, and our rancho has some interesting history about that, too.

Thar's Gold

Serious interest in gold mining on the Rancho San Vicente carried on for more than 60 years, right up into the 1930s. In fact, casual gold panning was still pursued as late as the 1980s during wet months in the San Vicente Creek and its tributaries. The names given to Klondike Creek and to Featherstone Canyon are testimony to the gold fever that pervaded the rancho in earlier days. The famous gold rush on the Klondike River in the Yukon Territory occurred in 1898 and influenced these names of places that remain today on the rancho.

However, nothing can be found in the records that would indicate anyone ever got rich from mining the grant lands, but, there always was that glimmer of hope, which kept people coming back and spending good time and money chasing the glitter.

The first written account of any success here appeared in the Feb. 13, 1874, edition of the San Diego Union. The article under the heading, "San Vicente Placers," tells about a call the paper received from a C. F. Weston. He had owned the Era House in San Diego, but sold out and went to the mountains to do some prospecting. The account goes on to say:

"It is well known to old residents of the county that gold exists in the vicinity of San Vicente and Santa Maria valleys; but hitherto we believe, no one has thought the deposits of sufficient importance to justify working. Mr. Weston and two companions have prospected the country pretty extensively and have opened two claims which they think will compare favorably with placer diggings anywhere. They took out over one hundred dollars worth of gold dust in less than two weeks, and that not by regular work, but by prospecting. Mr. Weston says he is satisfied that the gulches in which he is located will pay $2.50 to $3 per day to the man steadily washing with rockers and that the mines of San Vicente will prove to be a "bigger thing" than the Japa Placers in Lower California.

"A fine stream of water flows through the San Vicente valley, sufficient in volume to allow the employment of long-toms and sluices as well as the old-fashioned

rockers in working the dirt. The dirt from which Mr. Weston and company obtained the most of their gold is described as a blue gravel, although there is a great deal of red gravelly soil which also pay very well."

This article apparently set off a stampede for San Vicente. It also aroused the San Francisco owners of the rancho when they read the account of the Union article in their local paper. A letter to the editor of the Union appeared on March 15, 1874, and was signed simply, "San Vicente." It put the readers on notice that the San Vicente Rancho, which was surveyed by order of the U.S. Surveyor General, included the main creek, and that this survey was confirmed and a patent issued to Judge C. H. Chamberlain of San Francisco, legal trustee for the owners. This was private land and not subject to outsiders coming in and claiming mineral rights.

The letter further stated: "Personal notice of these facts was given to the party prospecting there in December by the writer, along with a copy of the official plat, containing the telegram from Washington when the patent had been issued." The party had been notified they could not permanently damage the surface or injure any growing timber. "A notice (printed on a board) was also nailed to a tree, by the side of the road crossing the valley from San Diego to Julian." Prospectors were told, however, that they could expect one-half interest in any mineral-bearing ledges they discovered.

The letter also said that "the San Vicente lands have been segregated. Sublett & Co. of El Cajon have leased for grazing the lands extending about six miles below and above the crossing of the Julian road."

McDonald & Co., real estate agents, who had been trying to peddle the land for the San Francisco speculators, now had an added attraction to tout. The following ad appeared in the San Diego Union on April 7, 1874:

SAN VICENTE PLACER MINES

Three Thousand Acres for
Sale at Moderate Prices
Title U. S. Patent
Fifteen Miles of Gulches.

These placer mines according to report of Prospectors
"will prove to be a bigger thing than the Japa Placers."

Only 30 Miles from San Diego
Immediate and Undisputed Possession Given
Apply
McDonald & Co., Agents

We don't know how effective the owners' notices were in controlling the mining or in protecting their property. We do know that the ad by McDonald & Co. didn't result in any land sales. It was nearly 10 years later before the land sold — and then it was not to prospectors, but to the solid farmers who eventually came and settled the valleys.

Other accounts of placer mining are found in

publications by the California State Mining Bureau. In 1914, Frederick J. H. Merrill, Ph.D., wrote:

> *BALLENA PLACER—This deposit of aquiferous gravel, lying southeast and east of Ramona and first described by H. W. Fairbanks as an old river bed with a southwesterly trend, belonging to a system of drainage now extinct and possibly of Tertiary age. The gold may have come from the region about Julian... these gravels have yielded values through a distance of 6 to 8 miles; the deposit probably extends south into the San Vicente Grant.*
>
> *The history and production of this placer are obscure. From the earliest times Mexicans and Indians have worked this gravel during the rainy season, when water was available, and there is no doubt that the production has been substantial. As often happens, some parts of this placer are quite rich and values of 1.50 or more per yard have been reported.*

During the 1920s, considerable money was invested in hydraulic placer mining on the west side of San Vicente Valley. Tailing piles are in evidence today at the base of the hill behind Oak Springs Drive where the operation took place. Water was pumped up from the San Vicente Creek to blast the gravel out of the hill and wash it on huge rockers. The equipment, however, kept breaking down, according to June Scarbery, daughter of John Mykrantz, who leased the land to the operators.

According to county records, Ballena Placers, Inc. recorded a mining lease in February 1926, but quitclaimed it on August 1927. San Vicente Placer Co. took up the lease the same month. State Division of Mines reports show that the Mykrantz land yielded but $14,500 in gold production between 1924 and 1930.

Klondike Creek, which is crossed by Wildcat Canyon Road about a mile south of San Vicente Road, was the site of panning activity that took place along its banks. Scars from hydraulic action can be detected today on the hills bordering the creek. James Barnett, grandson of Augustus Barnett, recalls that there was old rusting mine equipment still lying near the creek by the road up until World War II when it was hauled off for scrap.

There is no doubt that a considerable amount of gold has been taken by prospectors from the San Vicente area over the years. But there is no evidence that any one man, or group, got rich from mining the grant lands. In fact, considerably more money was spent over the years chasing the gold than has been warranted thus far.

San Vicente Copper

Another kind of mining took place on the San Vicente Rancho other than placer, and that was for copper at the Daley mine located on what is now the Monte Vista Ranch. Current U.S. Geological Survey maps show it spelled incorrectly as the "Daly Mine." While the mine showed traces of gold and silver, it yielded much more copper than it did the more precious metals, and more profit was made from copper than from gold.

Carlyle M. Daley, son of Thomas J. Daley, who

bought the Barona ranch in 1885, was interviewed by Edgar F. Hastings for the San Diego Historical Society in 1960:

> *"After my father acquired the Barona ranch he was driving over it to see what he had. He and Johnnie Boyd found a copper blowout and they left their tools there — a pick and a shovel — and came back into town. It was a month or so before they went out again. They couldn't find the location again and they never could find their pick and shovel, but they discovered another blowout. This blowout — surface ore — was similar to the United Verde Mine in Jerome, Arizona, which is probably one of the most famous copper mines in the world.*
>
> *"This blowout ore attracted many miners to the place and it sold several times but never stayed sold, we always got it back. Originally it sold to the Boston and Maine Company for $100,000 and a $1,500 deposit was collected. The last time it was sold was when I sold it in 1930 for $7,500 to two old men by the name of Ott and Lindsey. Lots of money was spent out there but no money at all ever taken off. The ore was pretty rich and kept getting richer all the time; however, they were a long ways from water level which they would have to be before they found out whether they had a copper mine or not.*
>
> *"As far as I know it is still out there — just a hole in the ground. If I remember right, the main shaft is down about 130 feet and from there tunnels are drilled off."*

Carlyle apparently did not know all there was to know about the operation of the Daley mine over the years. While it was not a roaring success, mining records show it was not a complete failure either.

Records indicate that in addition to the Boston and Maine Company, several other firms showed interest in the deposit, with varying degrees of success. A Feb. 13, 1900, item in the San Diego Union reported that articles of incorporation had been filed for the Barona Copper Mining & Smelting Co. the day before. The company was formed "for the purpose of developing the large ledge of copper on the Daley Ranch." If it proves out, they added, "Eastern capitalists will buy the mine." About three weeks later on March 4, the Union reported that the "sinking of a shaft began last week." Fine samples of copper were placed on display, they added, in the mining room of the San Diego Chamber of Commerce by Thomas Daley.

Between 1914 and 1919, the San Jacinto Mining & Milling Company worked the mine. Ore was smelted in a 50-ton reverberatory furnace. The total production was about 175,000 pounds of copper, of which about 150,000 pounds was produced in 1917 when, during World War I, the price of copper reached a peak of 27 cents per pound.

In 1924 (according to a recorded deed) George W. Lindsey purchased the property, which consisted of 100 acres, and leased it to the Southern California Mining and Milling Company. In 1928 he organized the Ramona Mining Company and sunk a shaft 113 feet deep into the outcrop and cut a working tunnel

200 feet into the side of the hill below the outcrop. Attempts were made to reclaim the ore developed from these cuts, but due to low metal prices and general apathy, the operation was closed down.

In 1935, Lindsey commissioned a rather extensive study, involving several expert geologists, to determine the economic feasibility of further operation of the mine. The study concluded that copper ore no longer was profitable and that success would depend upon finding consistent gold and silver values.

As an aside, one of the geologists involved in that study, James R. Evans, offered the following definition in his letter to the owners: "A geologist," he said, "is a fellow who tells you where ore is to be found and — when you don't find it — can explain in a scientific manner just why it wasn't there."

Apparently the ore wasn't there in sufficient values to justify the expense of reactivating the mine, for it has been idle since.

Today all that remains in evidence are some rotting timbers and, as Carlyle Daley put it, "just a hole in the ground."

The Buried Treasure

When this writer first came to San Vicente in 1970, one of the first things he heard was a pulse-elevating story about buried treasure, just waiting to be found, "right here on the ranch!" It is a story that persisted for at least 45 years, and fueled many a tortured man-hour of frenzied pick-and-shovel work.

In 1970, the site where all the interest was focused — on the side of the hill above Barona Mesa Road — looked like a battlefield, pock-marked by gaping holes of all sizes and shapes. As recently as the 1980s, a large Caterpillar bulldozer was employed to move thousands of cubic yards of rock and dirt in a vain search for the elusive fortune. Although the area is overgrown today, it still shows the wounds of all that evacuation.

In 1970, the tale was the subject of an 11-page cover story in a pulp magazine that featured treasure stories and metal detector ads.

The fable supposedly originated with an old bedridden Indian woman, who had first told it to her nephew some 70 years earlier. Years later, as a very old man, the nephew was ready to share the secret, and even put up $20 of his own limited funds to help finance an expedition.

His aunt told him how she had worked at a "mission" as a young girl. About once a week she was selected to go with other women into the hills to prepare meals for the padre and his Indian charges who were working a very rich silver mine. It seems that one day when she was back at the mission, she learned that much gold had arrived at their mission. The gold had been brought a great distance by mules and was to be held at the mission until a big ship came to take it away.

Shortly after, however, as the story goes, some kind of fighting broke out, and the padres gathered up all the gold and mission treasure for safekeeping. They loaded it in two oxcarts, and using burros, hauled it back up to the mine, along with an iron and oak mission door. The treasure was placed in the mine, the large door was put over the entrance, and all of it was covered with dirt.

The main clue to the location was a cross chiseled into a flat rock pointing to the mine entrance. The Indians were told, according to the story, that they would lose their souls if they ever returned to the mine. With that, they were carried off to the desert in Arizona.

After finishing her story, the old woman gave her nephew the approximate location of the mine, but refused to go there for fear, naturally, of losing her soul.

Nearly 70 years later, the expedition began. After weeks of search, markings were found on an old oak located where the golf course is now. These markings led to the cross-marked flat rock in a ravine above Barona Mesa Road.

For more than 20 years, so many holes were dug in this hill that it resembled a Hollywood battlefield set.

One of the principal diggers, a man who was obsessed with the project for more than 20 years, exhibited for illustration in the pulp journal two things that he claimed were found near the site: a Spanish pick with a wooden handle and a small mission bell with the year 1830 cast in it.

The story and description of the artifacts found have

been reviewed by historians who are experts in San Diego's past. As tempting as it is to want to believe in the existence of the lost treasure, unfortunately there is no factual historical basis for the legend. No Spanish plunder ever found its way to San Diego, and as one noted historian puts it, "The padres were as poor as church mice."

The location attributed to the legendary mine is not far from the main Diegueño village site near Barona Mesa Road. The small mission bell supposedly was found in a half-buried Indian pot. If such is true, the pot was no doubt a cremation urn, or olla, and the bell was a keepsake of its owner whose ashes were once in the pot.

As for the Spanish pick, if it really is genuine and had been lying there for more than 100 years, one has to wonder why the wooden handle had not been consumed by termites or brush fires long before the Indian aunt had time to get back from Arizona to start the mad treasure dig of San Vicente.

Backcountry, 1880s

THE DECADE OF THE 1880s brought solid settlers to San Vicente Valley. It was during this period that the neighboring settlement of Nuevo would take its present form, changing its name to Ramona. Pioneers with names such as Barnett, Dukes and Stockton would settle and be a part of the San Vicente and Ramona community for many years to come.

By the beginning of the decade, the County of San Diego had nearly doubled its 1870 population of 4,950 to more than 8,600. The State of California counted 865,000 people that year, more than two-thirds of whom resided in the northern part of the state. Only six cities in the whole state boasted populations of more than 10,000, and Southern California had but one — Los Angeles barely qualified with 11,300 citizens.

The City of San Diego tallied 2,637 in the census of 1880, but would experience a boom and bust in that decade, which saw a population of more than 40,000 in 1887 dwindle to 16,159 in 1890. The depression of 1888-89 took a heavy toll on the county's principal city.

The backcountry, on the other hand, saw a steady influx of farmers, orchardists, beekeepers and the like, accounting for a four-fold county growth to 34,987 by 1890. Much of this growth resulted from subdivision and promotion in the north and central parts of the county during the boom years of 1886 and 1887.

The Escondido Land and Town Company subdivided Rancho Rincon del Diablo into small farms and laid out a townsite. Rancho Penasquitos, the first of the area's Spanish land grants, was offered in tracts of 10 acres for $250 each. An added attraction was a lottery where the buyer put his name in a hat, with the first prize being a $25,000 Penasquitos ranch house then serving as a hotel.

In El Cajon Valley, a townsite was laid out by the El Cajon Valley Company.

Meanwhile, there were 18,000 sheep grazing on the Santa Maria Rancho, San Vicente's neighboring valley to the west. In 1883, Bernard Etcheverry produced 75,000 pounds of high-grade wool, keeping 50 shearers busy.

But with the land boom, and the growing pressure for smaller tracts of land, the Santa Maria Rancho, too, was soon broken up. A group of promoters, headed by Milton Santee of Los Angeles, came to Nuevo and in May 1886 acquired some 7,000 acres. In August, the Santa Maria Land and Water Company was incorporated

THIS ADVERTISEMENT APPEARED in the March 4, 1887, edition of the San Diego Union for lots and parcels offered by the Santa Maria Land and Water Company. The town of Nuevo was subdivided and renamed Ramona. Lots on Main Street 100 feet wide were priced at $100, and 80-foot lots on other streets went for $50.

FRIDAY MORNING, MARCH 4, 1887

REAL ESTATE

RAMONA!

Santa Maria Ranche.

San Diego County, Cal.

The Gem Ranche of San Diego County—Pure Water—Pure Air—Fine
Seminary—Good Hotel—Finest Vineyard Soil in Southern
California, and the Choicest Spot for
Deciduous Fruits.

THE RANCHE.

The Santa Maria Land and Water Company have subdivided and now offer for sale 7,000 acres of the choicest land in San Diego county.

RAMONA.

In the center of the tract a town has been laid out and called Ramona, and a Postoffice established thereon, the name of Nuevo Postoffice having been changed to Ramona by order of the Postoffice Department. Ramona is thirty miles from San Diego, on the line of the proposed extension of the Southern Pacific Railroad from Dos Palmas to San Diego, and the line of the proposed extension of California Southern from Oceanside. The present means of communication is by a daily line of four-horse Concord coaches.

RAINFALL.

The advantage of this Colony above all others established in San Diego county is that it lies upon the second rain belt of the county, which has an average of double the rainfall of any part of the Coast counties, and in dry years is always certain to produce full crops.

CLIMATE.

Ramona is situated 1,800 feet above the sea level, 25 miles from the Coast and above the line of fog; no dew falls, so that the air both during the day and night is absolutely free from dampness. One may sleep upon the ground in open air without the slightest fear of contracting a cold. No place in the country is there so perfectly protected a spot from ocean fogs. Asthma sufferers here find a perfect relief from their terrible sufferings, and if there is a cure for consumption or bronchial complaints, it is to be found here.

WATER AND SOIL.

Cold, sparkling springs of soft granite water abound, while well water can be obtained at not more than 25 feet on any portion of the tract. In addition, we have a water right in Santa Maria Creek that will be piped to the town of Ramona, thus insuring an ample water supply at all times and all seasons.

The soil is that rich, red loam so highly prized by the wine-makers of Napa and Sonoma counties. This, in connection with the fact that no irrigation is needed, makes it one of the choicest spots in California for vineyards.

The elevation of Santa Maria gives it an advantage over the lowlands in summer climate, and also in the raising of deciduous fruits, and all other products which along the Coast are deficient in that flavor peculiar to the East.

ADVANTAGES.

The University of Southern California will build and establish a Seminary in the town of Ramona that in time will attain a high place among the educational institutions of the country. Buildings costing $50,000 are to be erected on the site selected on an eminence overlooking the valley. The Seminary is endowed with ample funds for its support. Work to commence in six months. Hence those unfortunate, suffering with pulmonary and other afflictions having families, have the assurance that not only will they get relief from their troubles, but their families will not be deprived of cultured associations by making their homes here.

A fine hotel, now being constructed, will be conducted in a homelike manner and at reasonable rates, affording ample accommodations to those who wish to view the ranche and remain to test the climate and satisfy themselves of the desirability of Ramona as a home for

Health, Education, Pleasure and Profit.

All purchasers of land in the ranche or lots in the town of Ramona will be transported free of charge from San Diego to Ramona and return.

PRICE.

Lots, 50x140 feet, 20-foot alleys; Blocks 200x500 20-foot alleys.
Main street, 100 feet wide; other streets 80 feet wide.
Price of lots on Main street, $100; corner, $200; other streets, $50; corners on other streets, $100.
Five, ten, twenty and forty-acre tracts at $20 to $50 per acre.
TERMS: One-third cash; balance in one and two years, with interest at seven per cent per annum on deferred payments. Five per cent off for cash.
For maps and information, call on or address

SANTA MARIA LAND AND WATER CO.,

MILTON SANTEE,
President and Manager,
964 Fifth St., San Diego.

DIRECTORS.	OFFICERS.
MILTON SANTEE,	MILTON SANTEE, President.
WM. H. GOUCHER,	W. H. GOUCHER, Vice-President.
THOS. FESSENDEN,	R. A. THOMAS, Treasurer.
R. A. THOMAS,	N. G. DOW, Secretary.
LEVI CHASE,	

RAMONA'S TOWN HALL is shown here in 1894, shortly after Augustus Barnett donated it to the community. The banner across the front says, 'Welcome To The Santa Maria Valley, Railroad Connection With San Diego.' Three different railroads talked about building to Ramona, but none ever got that far.

and capitalized at $100,000, with $92,000 already subscribed on the filing date. The other incorporators were Thomas Fessenden and William Goucher of Los Angeles, R. A. Thomas of San Diego and Julius Finch of San Francisco.

A company ad, appearing on March 4, 1887, in the San Diego Union, extolled the boundless virtues of the "Santa Maria Ranche." Why 'rancho' was spelled 'ranche' throughout the ad is a mystery. It was, they said, "The Gem Ranche of San Diego County — Pure Water Pure Air — Fine Seminary — Good Hotel — Finest Vineyard Soil in Southern California, and the Choicest

Spot for Deciduous Fruits."

Potential buyers were told Ramona would soon be "on the line of the proposed extension of the Southern Railroad from Dos Palmas to San Diego, and the proposed extension of the California Southern from Oceanside." The ad went on to say, "The University of Southern California will build and establish a Seminary in the town of Ramona that in time will attain a high place among the educational institutions of the country. Buildings costing $50,000 are to be erected on the site selected on an eminence overlooking the valley. The seminary is endowed with ample funds for its support. Work to commence in six months. Hence those unfortunates, suffering with pulmonary and other afflictions having families, have the assurance that not only will they get relief from their troubles, but their families will not be deprived of cultured associations by making their homes here."

Lots that were 50 feet by 140 feet with 20-foot alleys were priced at $100 on Main Street and at $50 on other streets. Five-, 10-, 20- and 40-acre tracts were priced at $20 to $50 per acre. "TERMS: One-third cash; balance in one and two years, with interest at seven percent per annum on deferred payments. Five percent off for cash."

The railroads never made it to Ramona, nor was the grand seminary built there. (It was built in Escondido instead.) But the people came, and in time, the lots and parcels sold anyway.

RAMONA FOLKS hadn't see anything like the Santa Maria Land and Water Company's land sale promotion of 1887 until Ray Watt topped it by starting sales of more than 3,000 lots and 400 condominiums for the San Diego Country Estates. Above is the sales kick-off ad that appeared in the San Diego Union on Aug. 4, 1972.

San Vicente's Pioneer Settlers

WHILE SOUTHERN CALIFORNIA was booming with new settlements springing up all over San Diego's backcountry, San Vicente remained pretty much as it always had been — off the main road and sparsely populated.

Of all the early San Vicente settlers, Augustus Barnett is perhaps better known today than any other because of a legacy he left to the community — the Ramona Town Hall.

It became apparent to Augustus after living here awhile that Nuevo needed a meeting place. In 1893 he did something about it. The San Diego Union of July 31, 1893, reported:

> "Work was commenced last Tuesday in Nuevo on the Barnett Hall and Library, a free gift to the town by A. Barnett, a public-spirited citizen of Santa Maria Valley. With the building, which is to cost $10,000, will be donated a public library of 5,000 volumes. The structure will be composed of adobe and veneer

*of pressed brick being 22 inches in thickness.
Surrounding the hall, a park is to be tastefully
laid out by Milton Santee, who donated the site
for the building.*"

And on Feb. 9, 1894, the Union stated:

*"The town of Nuevo is making grand preparations
to celebrate Washington's birthday by dedication of
its new town hall and library, the public-spirited
gift of Augustus Barnett. San Diego music and
dramatic talent will be on hand and the entire
population of that section is bound to make the
occasion memorable.*"

The original deed to the community stated the hall
was to be used "for a library, museum, dances and other
entertainment." It was donated to the townspeople of
Nuevo on Washington's birthday Feb. 22, 1894 — a
year before the town was officially renamed Ramona.

The town hall is held in trust in perpetuity by a
volunteer five-member board of trustees. It is not
owned by the trustees, nor by any public agency. For
more than 118 years it has operated solely on private
donations, grant money and rent collected from public
and commercial tenants. The fact that it is still serving
the public over these many years is a tribute not only
to the quality of its construction, but to generations of
public-spirited trustees. For many years, in recent times,
leaders such as W.T. "Woodie" Kirkman, and Darrell and
Jacqueline Beck, have continually helped to maintain

A HUNTING PARTY gathers on front porch of the Barnett's ranch house during the late 1890s. Mr. Barnett is standing on the far left and Martha Barnett is seated in the back row, next to him.

and restore it.

William Augustus Barnett was born in Cherry Valley, N.Y., in 1817 into a prominent family. His father, Melancton, moved his family to Cleveland in 1825 where he became a well-respected businessman. His brother, James, later took over his father's banking and merchant business and also served in the Union Army, reaching the rank of Brigadier General of the 7th Ohio Regiment during the Civil War.

In 1850, when Augustus was in his early 30s, he was lured to the California gold fields and was listed in the El Dorado County census as a "miner." He returned east within a year, however. But by April 1870, he was still attracted to California, so he and his wife, Martha, moved their family west via the first transcontinental railroad, the Union Pacific. "That was the spring after they drove the golden spike," according to grandson James Barnett, "and few trains got through to California during that first winter due to heavy snows."

The Barnetts settled in San Jose, and then moved to San Diego five years later. Augustus soon discovered San Vicente and acquired his first parcel of land situated between the Santa Maria and San Vicente grant lines and filed for a homestead. To that he added two adjoining parcels and soon had a 1,100-acre ranch on which he farmed, ran cattle and raised bees.

In 1885, he built the original large adobe ranch house, which stands today with its 13-foot high ceilings and its wide verandas shading three sides. It has one of the first solar hot water systems in the county, installed by Augustus' son, Melancton, in 1914, and in good working order today. The ranch house is located just west of the San Vicente grant line south of San Vicente Road at the point where it bends east and drops into the valley.

In 1884 Augustus purchased three parcels in the San Vicente grant from one of the parties in the San Francisco syndicate. One parcel was located in the extreme north end of the valley, in the vicinity of where Rutherford Road is today. Another was situated in the western valley, where the wastewater treatment plant stands, while the third was where the eastern part of the San Vicente Golf Course is located. The total consideration for the 853 acres contained in the three parcels was $2,230, or $2.61 per acre. He gave a note to the seller for $1,000, due in one year and bearing interest at 12%.

MARTHA BARNETT, founder and benefactor of Ramona's (Nuevo's) first library. She and husband Augustus saw to it that a cultural foundation was set in place by donating a library with a respectable collection as part of their new Town Hall.

AUGUSTUS BARNETT is shown as a banker and real estate investor in the 1870s, wearing a suit with a gold watch chain — a very different image from the man Nuevo folks knew, as shown with a hunting party on page 111.

While this land price sounds extremely cheap by today's standards, consider the era. These were times when a well-to-do family of five lived on $500 a year. The land was semi-desert with no source for irrigation, and the terms of the loan were not very favorable. His up-front cash payment of $1,230 would equate to about $150,000 today.

In 1887 he traded the two disconnected parcels located in the central part of the valley for land owned by Stockton and Dukes, which abutted his parcel in the western valley. He thus assembled about 1,300 contiguous acres. The 500 or so acres of beautiful meadowland bisected by the San Vicente Creek, east of Wildcat Canyon Road, running to a point south of Spangler Peak, he named "Creekside." According to Ramona historian Guy Woodward, Augustus is said to have stated, "There's a Lakeside and a Riverside, so why not a Creekside."

Augustus built a large earthen dam, and remnants of it can be seen today, across from and just east of the wastewater plant. Augustus planted vineyards, oranges and lemons, irrigating them by gravity flow from the dam. He erected a brick packing house near the grove to prepare his fruit for market. Grandson James tells a story that illustrates the pride Augustus had in the farm:

"One year there was a crop failure — no oranges. So he spent a whole day tying mock orange gourds onto those trees to look like oranges so people wouldn't know they didn't have oranges." Two relic trees were still there and producing a few oranges into the 1980s.

A good deal of Augustus' efforts were turned to raising bees. Much of the ranch's income was derived from production and marketing of wild buckwheat and sage honey. It is said he was one of the top producers and shippers of honey from San Diego County by the end of the 20th century.

JAMES BARNETT (right) is shown in 1982 with Ramona historian Guy Woodward. The family's large adobe ranch house (below) stands today much as it did when it was first built in 1885.

Barnett Ranch Today

When we started San Diego Country Estates (SDCE) in 1970, the Barnett Ranch was owned by James Barnett, grandson of Augustus. James' primary residence was in Pasadena, where he ran a chainsaw marketing business, but he drove down to the ranch most every weekend. At that time the total ranch consisted of the old adobe house and about 1,100 contiguous acres. Included was Creekside area and land north of San Vicente Road where the water reclamation plant and Vicente Meadows are now. That area was bought by SDCE developer Ray Watt to build the reclamation facilities that he later conveyed to the San Vicente Sanitation District. The Creekside land south of San Vicente Road was later sold by Watt and subdivided by others into four-acre parcels where beautiful homes have since been built along Tombill Road.

James died in 1991, and after conducting several studies, his heirs decided to retain the old adobe home and 100 acres. Today that estate is owned, farmed and occupied by James' grandson, Phillip Parker, and his wife, Clair. The remaining 732 acres were sold in 2002 to the County of San Diego and placed in a Multiple Species Conservation Program called the Barnett Ranch Preserve. There are four miles of trails and a staging area open to the public, located just south of San Vicente Road.

While Augustus is remembered by the community as a prosperous and successful farmer, it appears much of his fortune was amassed from real estate and finance. His brother, James Barnett, was president of the First National Bank of Cleveland and the two of them were investment partners right up into the 1890s, in at least one office building. Additionally, Augustus was quite active as a local moneylender.

County Warrents (In Tin Box)					
Date	Name	No.	Amt.	Interest From	
1882					
Nov. 24	T. Larson	817	$4.	12-2-82	Service as juror
Dec. 2	C.S. Hamilton	918	132.	12-2-82	Allowance to indigents
1883					
Jan. 11	G.W. B. McDonald	60	22.	1-11-83	Lumber for poor farm
1884					
Jan. 19	E. W. Bushyhead	54	464.13	1-21-84	Boarding prisoners
Apl. 18	S. D. Union	250	931.05	4-18-84	Pub. of delinquent tax list
1885					
Jan. 26	Hinton & Gordon	150	1.50	5-4-85	Hay for bed ticks

During that era, it was the practice of the County of San Diego to pay its claims for goods and services with warrants. These claims would be assigned to banks or private money lenders who would pay off the claimants' warrants and then collect from the county, with interest, after the property tax revenue was collected. Barnett was one of those who purchased these warrants. Such typical claims are listed in his account book as follows:

A notation at the bottom of his ledger read, "After May 14, 1883 Warrents (sic) bear but 5% Int., all before that time drew 7%."

Barnett also lent money to individuals. Among his clients were men well known in the San Diego

A PICNIC SCENE AT CREEKSIDE in about 1898. The setting is on present-day Tombill Road, next to the San Vicente Creek, across from the water reclamation plant.

community, such as G. W. Marston. He lent to his neighbors Dukes, Stockton, Poole and Haworth, and the loans were secured by mortgages against their lands. Such loans typically ranged from $350 to $1,000 for a term of two years, with interest at 10% per year.

James Barnett recalls a story John Barger told him during the 1930s about one of Augustus' loans. "Seems Barger as a young man was in need of $100 and went to see my grandfather. Augustus agreed to loan him the money but neither of them had a blank check, whereupon, my grandfather reached up, pulled off a shingle from the shed they were standing under and proceeded to write that check on the wooden shingle. Amazingly," said Jim, "the bank cashed the wooden check. John told me 50 years after the incident he'd give $100 cash to have that shingle back as a souvenir."

Augustus Barnett was a driving force in the community for nearly a quarter century. He died in his 90th year, in June 1906.

The Dukes

The Dukes name is another one closely associated with the San Vicente Valley and the Ramona community for nearly 90 years. The first of that family to settle here was James Dukes, a native of Illinois.

He had come across the plains and mountains in an oxcart at age 16, settling in the Stockton-Antioch area in 1850. He was nearly 50, and still a bachelor when he decided to pull up stakes and move to Southern California. He found San Vicente Valley land for sale, liked what he saw and bought an undivided half interest in about 2,000 acres from Judge Chamberlain in 1883.

In the spring of 1885, he talked his good friend and former Antioch neighbor, James Stockton, into purchasing the other half interest and the two went into partnership. The Stockton-Dukes ranch covered much of that area developed as San Diego Country Estates (SDCE) west of Ramona Oaks. They grazed cattle and raised barley in a partnership that lasted 10 years. In 1894 the San Diego Union told of its dissolution: "Mr. Stockton takes the upper half and Mr. Dukes, the Lower."

In the meantime, James Dukes' brother, William, and family were in South Dakota. During the winter of 1891, James encouraged his brother to come west. While they left some bitter winters behind, they were to find that San Diego County, in the midst of an extended drought, offered its own brand of harshness.

The William Dukes family bought 160 acres of land just east of where Ramona Oaks Park is now. When the family moved to San Vicente, there were two children, James and Val. Val died of meningitis at age 3, shortly after arriving here. His grave was situated on a hill in the vicinity of the present Cathedral Way and was moved to the Nuevo Cemetery in 1974 before development took place in that part of SDCE.

While James, the first of the Dukes to settle in the valley, had no children and died in 1898 at age 64, another James, "Jimmy" Dukes, his nephew, is better remembered today. He was a community leader for more than 50 years. Just 5 years old when the family moved west, Jimmy was a most active citizen of the Ramona area until he died at age 84 in 1970.

William and wife, Celestine Dukes, would have three more children born in the Ramona area — Fred, John and Mary. Mary (Walters) is well remembered as one of the last telephone operators in the area. Ramona was the last manual telephone exchange in PT&T's Southern California operation when they converted to dial service in 1960.

Backcountry life was especially rough in the early 1890s. Not only was the nation in a depression, but the drought made farming impossible, and little feed could be raised for livestock. William Dukes supported his family by cutting oak wood, with the help of local Indians, and hauling it to San Diego where he sold it door to door. The San Vicente Valley, near the creek, was a veritable forest of trees in those early days. Areas, such as those where the golf course is today, were vast oak groves.

"Jimmy" recalled in an interview for the San Diego Historical Society in 1959, "We raised just enough fruit for the family use — a home orchard. We had peaches and apricots, and plums. They did fine."

After a few years, the family established a new home

BROTHERS JAMES AND WILLIAM DUKES. Bachelor James came to San Vicente in 1883. William (right) followed with his family, moving to 160 acres in the eastern part of the valley eight years later.

where Vista Ramona Drive now meets the Old Julian Road, so as to be closer to school for the children. Mary Walters remembers the family referring to those times in the San Vicente Valley as "hard scrabble."

Jimmy and brother, Fred, while still teenagers, ran a threshing crew, working the various valleys in the area. Jimmy later became a member of the Ramona School Board and served for 42 years. In the 1959 interview, he told how he first was elected to the board in 1911: "I had a ranch down there by the schoolhouse, and I was out there working in the field. A couple of fellows came over and wanted me to come over. They said they were having a school election. So I went over, green, didn't know what was happening. They didn't have the ballots then. They'd just sit around a public meeting and then they'd call for a vote. They never nominated anybody. So when I got out, I found I was a Trustee. They just worked me, worked me in there. I kept with it a long time."

Jimmy Dukes was the first master of the Ramona Grange, established in 1914, and said to be the first grange in Southern California.

Jimmy also gave an insight on jails and trials in the area at the turn of the century: "Of course, those days a trial always brought a big crowd. One time one of the fellows by the name of Ray Clevenger was working for Billy Warnock on the threshing crew. He pulled a knife on Billy and they had him arrested. Jim Haworth was the constable. He went out and arrested him. They had a little old iron jail down there (Ramona). He wouldn't put him in it because he was afraid it would get too hot

JAMES DUKES is shown here in later years, as a Ramona School Board Trustee, a post he held for 42 years.

JIMMY DUKES (third from right) is shown with a thrashing crew in front of their cookhouse. Brother Fred is on far right. The photo was taken during the early 1900s.

in there in the middle of summertime, so they had their trial. Everybody in the neighborhood came in to it. The judge was Judge Sloan, the father of the attorney Sloan. That was about 1900 or 1899, about in there. They acquitted him, he went off. They let him loose. They gave him a scolding, told him not to do it anymore."

James Haworth

The man who was the constable at the time of that episode was James W. Haworth, another early San Vicente settler. The Haworth family owned and lived on the 120 acres located in the northeast corner of the valley. Several large eucalyptus trees still guard the old Haworth homestead at the north end of Daza Drive today. Haworth served as the area constable from 1895 to 1901.

The Ramona constable in those days had a lot of area to police. The territory took in all the Santa Maria Valley, Ballena, Santa Ysabel, Warner Springs, Julian, Borrego and Oak Grove.

The Stocktons

James Stockton was 60 years old when he decided to move south to join his friend Dukes in 1884. He had served 20 years as a customs official in San Francisco. The family had been farming 320 acres in Antioch for 17 years when their home was lost to fire.

His wife, Susan Layne Stockton, with their eight children, ages 8 to 17, moved south a year later. The San Diego Union, on July 28, 1885, reported: "Mr. James Stockton, of the San Francisco Customs House, has lately

THE STOCKTON HOUSE as it appeared about 1889. It was located on the north side of what is now Wikiup Road, near Republican Way.

bought land in the San Vicente Rancho, near Nuevo; his family came overland from San Francisco reaching their new home last week." The trip took 31 days. Their first home, a 20-by-24-foot wood frame house, was located on the north side of Wikiup Road and a few hundred feet north of where Republican Way is today.

When the developers of SDCE started to build the half-mile training track at the equestrian center in 1973, the streets and water system were not yet constructed in that area. We were in need of a nearby source of water for grading and compacting the track, and we happened to mention this fact to Dorace Scarbery. He recalled that while on horseback looking for stray cattle some years earlier, he nearly fell into an old overgrown well in the area.

Fred Harris and the author set off to find the well.

SHOWN ON THEIR 50ᵀᴴ wedding anniversary in 1941 are James Shanklin Stockton and his wife, Lydia. As a teenager, he moved with the family from Antioch to the San Vicente Valley in 1885.

After some considerable beating of brush, we stumbled onto the rock foundation of the old Stockton farmhouse. Fred went downhill in one direction and I in another, and in no time Fred let out a yell. There it was, covered with brush, a neat rock-lined well 3 feet in diameter. We dropped a stone and heard a splash about 30 feet down. We had found the water we needed for construction, as well as a source to fill the infield lake and to operate the entire horse facility for a couple of years.

The well had to be abandoned later when it was discovered that it fell smack-dab in the middle of the planned intersection of Wikiup Road and Republican Way. We mused, not knowing anything then of the history of the homestead, or the hardships those early settlers put up with by comparison with conditions today. Imagine having to carry all your household water

THESE ARTIFACTS were excavated from the site of the Stockton's home. The lead soldier was a toy of one of the eight Stockton children.

by bucket 200 feet uphill. Probably nobody had to be reminded about water conservation in that household.

The Stocktons lived, farmed and raised cattle there until 1899. Several years of below average rainfall had developed into a serious drought, cutting into crop production and range feed for grazing. To compound that bleak situation, a form of meningitis struck, taking its toll of the weakened cattle. The family picked up and moved to the Dehesa area.

They returned to the valley, however, in 1906, some taking up residency in Ramona where the Stockton name was prominent for more than a half century. The family owned considerable acreage in the valley up until 1911 when Susan Layne Stockton sold it to Fiorezo Moretti.

The Morettis

Fiorezo Moretti had immigrated to the United States from Switzerland in the early 1900s and purchased the Stockton Ranch in order to start a dairy operation.

When the author first saw the San Vicente Valley in

A COMBINE AND CREW work in a barley field at the base of Spangler Peak in about 1912.

1970, the ruins of the old Moretti barns and milking facilities were still very much in evidence. The operation was located on the land that is now the fourth fairway on the golf course, south of the corner of San Vicente and Gunn Stage Roads.

Victor Cauzza of Santa Ysabel was a 16-year old farmhand when he worked for the Morettis in 1921. According to Victor, the Morettis "raised pigs and calves — that was the main thing at the time." While they milked nearly one hundred head, they sold no milk. The cream was separated out and sent to market while the skim milk was fed to the pigs. "They also raised a lot of grain," said Victor.

The Morettis sold the ranch to John Mykrantz in 1922. Fiorezo, his wife, Erma Linda, and two brothers, Philippe and Felix, bought the Santa Ysabel Ranch and moved their efficient Swiss operation 15 miles northeast.

JAMES POOLE is shown with a prized saddle horse, in about 1910.

The Pooles

In addition to the Morettis, the new century brought the Poole name to the western San Vicente Valley.

Bees and the commercial production of honey was big business during those times. San Vicente Valley provided an ideal area for high production. With thousands of acres of black sage and wild buckwheat, the prolific bees produced some of the finest honey in the world. It is said that honey from the San Vicente and Santa Maria Valleys was highly prized for its superior flavor. Most of this local product was shipped to Europe, with Belgium being the principal importer.

Most ranchers in the area kept at least a few stands of bees, taking advantage of one of the few cash crops of the day. Not only were the family table's needs met, but the excess supply was a fine source of ready money during those Spartan times. The big commercial producers in the area were James Poole and Augustus Barnett of San Vicente and James Kerr of Ramona.

James Barnett recalled, "Bill Robinson told me many years ago that my grandfather (Augustus) shipped 30 tons of honey out of here in one year — that's a lot of honey." Based on 100 to 150 pounds per stand, Augustus must have maintained about 400 to 600 bee stands.

In 1907, James and Minnie Poole bought 160 acres next to the San Vicente Creek. They had lived in Ramona for about 15 years. They moved to their new ranch located just southwest of Creekside in order to take advantage of the marvelous resources that virgin area offered the apiarist.

The Pooles raised a large family on their San Vicente Ranch. Their family reunions and big get-togethers with friends and neighbors were always major social events.

Mrs. Minnie Poole is remembered by Sam Quincey as "very much of a lady — but also very strong." Sam recalled seeing her, while she was in her 70s, routinely picking up and carrying two 5-gallon cans of honey at the same time. Their San Vicente place stayed in Poole ownership until 1944 when Minnie sold it to Mayme Brown.

Early Barona Ranchers

WHILE SAN VICENTE VALLEY was being settled during the 1880s, the Barona Valley was catching the eye and imagination of an enterprising San Diego promoter. He was Thomas J. Daley, who came west shortly after Mrs. O'Leary's cow caused so much damage in Chicago.

Thomas' son, Carlyle, told the San Diego Historical Society in 1960:

> "After the fire of 1872 my father and his mother left Chicago and came to San Diego by way of the Isthmus of Panama, shipping their household goods around the Horn. The thing that attracted my grandmother and my father to San Diego was once when they were walking down the street in Chicago they saw in a real estate office window a map of Point Loma covered with coconut trees and monkeys. They went in to find out what this was and someone sold them a gold mine."

As it developed, the gold mine was located in Baja

California, not San Diego. Like most such ventures, it turned out to be a waste of time for Daley. Upon finally settling in Old Town, Daley went into the business of manufacturing Chinese matches. "The matches would come in little square blocks of wood and you would break them off and carry a few in your vest pocket," Carlyle said. "Anyone who remembers the matches can remember the terrible stink they used to make. They had sulphur on them and would smell like the dickens!"

Daley moved from matches to abstracts in the early 1880s, forming one of the first title companies in San Diego. "There was no guarantee of title to property in those days," Carlyle said. "They just gave you an abstract of the title with a stack of papers and you took those to your attorney and took his OK on it."

When the land boom started in 1885, the real estate firm of Reed, Daley and Gassen was formed. It was about this time that Thomas Daley acquired the Barona Ranch and most of the Monte Vista Ranch, as well. This feat required the assembly of nearly 50 parcels with more than a dozen ownerships involved.

Daley envisioned starting a model community by selling the land in small parcels at reasonable prices and furnishing the settlers a few head of cattle, some fruit trees and implements at a low cost. However, the land bubble broke in 1889, followed by the panic of 1893, so his dream never became a reality. Instead, the Barona Valley became the setting for a large grain and cattle ranch. At one time, it is said, Daley had 60 men working in the grain and hay operations. Daley also had an ostrich farm, which attracted considerable attention at the ranch.

FOSTER DEPOT, the eastern terminus for the San Diego, Cuyamaca and Eastern Railroad, as it was in 1911. Foster is located just south of where the San Vicente Dam now stands. The stagecoach finished the trip from San Diego to Ramona, winding north on the Mussey Grade Road, through where the reservoir now is, and on up into the Santa Maria Valley.

Thomas Daley was one of the organizers of the San Diego, Cuyamaca and Eastern Railway Company (SDC&E). The principal organizer was Robert W. Waterman, who was governor of California from 1887 to 1891. Waterman had made his fortune from the Barstow Mine, taking out $1.6 million in silver between 1880 and 1887. He was elected lieutenant governor in 1886 and became governor in September 1887 upon the death of Gov. Washington Bartlett. Waterman purchased the Cuyamaca Rancho and reopened the Stonewall Mine, one of the richest gold producers in Julian. Daley was also a partner with Waterman in the Stonewall Mine.

133

The SDC&E Railroad was organized in 1887 and built in 1888-89. It started at the foot of N Street in San Diego and ran 23 miles through Lemon Grove, La Mesa and Lakeside, terminating at the Foster railroad station. This depot was located just below the present San Vicente Dam, where the old Mussey Grade Road used to come out of the hills from Ramona. Carlyle Daley reminisced in 1960:

"When they were building the San Diego and Cuyamaca Railroad, the people who owned all around El Cajon, the Boston and Maine Company — known locally as the Bostonians — wouldn't give land to the railroad for the right of way. Most everybody else gave their land to the railroad and were glad to do it to get the railroad out there. But these people wouldn't and in retaliation the railroad cut the City of El Cajon off the main track and just skirted it, making a big bend in the foothills to keep from going close to El Cajon Valley.

"What I am wondering now, and always have wondered, is how they expected to get that railroad out of Foster where it went right up to a dead end. The railroad was supposed to go through Barona Valley and up to the mine at Julian, however, they were all broke before the railroad was finished. But I don't think that there is even a locomotive today that is powerful enough to pull a train up that grade to Cuyamaca."

Thomas Daley served as general manager of the railroad for a while, but was bought out by Waterman in 1890 in one of the company's many reorganizations.

The SDC&E played a big role in the dreams and expectations of the people in Ramona, Santa Ysabel and Mesa Grande. The railroad, never being a big moneymaker, did agree in 1892 to extend its service to these communities in return for their guarantee of $100,000 in freight earnings. Several campaigns were jointly launched by the Ramona and San Diego Chambers of Commerce to get the tracks extended into the backcountry.

The San Diego Union is replete with reports from 1892 to 1909 about the efforts of the backcountry leaders to get the railroad up the hill. Some of the men most prominent in these efforts were T. P. Converse, Charles L. Slone and Joseph H. Kerr. But the required capital was never raised, and the railroad to Ramona remained only a dream.

Even so, the line to Foster made it possible for Ramonans to get to San Diego and back in one day. This trip required the traveler to be out at five o'clock in the morning to ride the four-horse stage of Frary and Fosters down the Mussey Grade to catch the train from Foster.

In 1897, Thomas Daley sold the main part of his grant-land holdings, some 2,700 acres encompassing the Barona Ranch, to James E. Wadham.

Wadham, a prominent San Diego attorney, was later to serve as mayor of that city from 1911 to 1913. He had built a beautiful home at 7th and Ash but rented it and moved to Barona Valley for health reasons upon acquiring the Daley ranch. The Wadhams ran a large cattle operation for the five years they owned the ranch.

Besides being a good lawyer and mayor, James Wadham distinguished himself in yet another way. According to the San Diego Union of Sept. 11, 1920, Wadham, as a boy

THE JAMES WADHAM FAMILY is shown in front of their Barona ranch house in 1899. The house stood until 1976 when it was lost to fire.

in the early 1880s, carried all the newspapers that were delivered in San Diego.

In 1903 Wadham sold his Barona landholdings to William H. Jones, then president of the International Harvesting Machinery Company. Total consideration for the 2,700 acres was $38,000, or $14 an acre.

Jones, who lived in Chicago, turned the property over to his son, Hugh Jones Jr., who made his home there. He was engaged in breeding valuable horse and cattle stock and in some testing of farm equipment.

THE JONES BARONA RANCH HOUSE was being used as the Barona Tribal headquarters when this picture was taken with tribal chairman Clifford LaChappa in 1997.

The Jones heirs owned the ranch up until shortly before it was acquired by the U.S. government in 1932 as part of the Barona Indian Reservation. The shell of the Jones' spacious adobe ranch house still stands today, and is used for tribal council business. It can be seen from Wildcat Canyon Road, situated just north of the Barona Community Center.

Latter-Day Pioneers

JOHN MYKRANTZ FIRST SAW the San Vicente Valley in 1921 when Harry Weiss invited him down to see his polo pony ranch, which we know today as Ramona Oaks. Mykrantz had earlier purchased Weiss' home in Los Angeles, and the two had become good friends.

According to June Mykrantz Scarbery, his daughter, he returned home from that trip to announce to his wife, Elizabeth, that he had bought a ranch. "He had been bored from the front porch to the back porch," added June, "and he was looking for something to keep busy with."

His new acquisition was the Moretti ranch, and it was to be the first of many purchases he made of San Vicente land. Over the next few years, John Mykrantz would acquire about 7,000 acres, more than half of the total of three square leagues contained in the old rancho boundary.

Mykrantz, an attorney, had amassed his fortune as a real estate developer and investor. His initial stake was made in the industrial cities of Ohio during the early part of the century, building apartment flats for workers and renting them for $5 per month. He came to California in 1911 and parlayed this money into greater wealth from property investments in South Gate and Ventura.

Mykrantz had little interest in the mundane aspects of farming. When he realized he had acquired a going dairy operation with the ranch, he told his wife he'd just have to give the dairy away. According to June, "My mother told him in no uncertain terms that if he was to give it to anyone, it would be to her. She took it over in 1922 and ran it until Scar and I took it over in 1938."

When we came to the valley in 1970, the old cow barns were in ruins, located on the present-day 13th fairway of the San Vicente Golf Course.

What really did interest John Mykrantz, however, was the opportunity he saw for developing a vast irrigation system that would fully exploit the valley's potential. He envisioned a series of dams that would catch and impound much of the water that flowed through the San Vicente Creek from the eastern valley's 48 square miles of watershed.

He hired Thomas King, a former water engineer with the City of San Diego, to design the system. Each water course coming into the valley would have two dams — the first, a check dam that would spill over into the next dam, which would serve as a small reservoir. A large main dam was built at the west end of the main valley, the ruins of which are in prominent evidence today.

"The problem with the system," according to June Scarbery, "was that many of the tributary dams sanded

JOHN MYKRANTZ (right) is shown with a prized catch on Catalina in 1921, the same year he acquired the San Vicente Valley ranch.

up during the first rainy season, and the rest washed out in the big flood of 1927."

During 1922-23 Mykrantz invested a small fortune in the program. He spent $125,000 cash on concrete and labor for the big dam alone. A.B. Elliott of Ramona recalled for the author that the dam construction provided a big boost to the local economy at the time. He was one who worked on the big dam and was able, he said, to save enough money to go back to Duchess County, New York, to marry his wife, Ruth.

According to Elliott, the concrete was mixed in gasoline-powered cement mixers and poured by wheelbarrows. "It took two men to each wheelbarrow. Had a man in front with a rope and hook, called him the mule, and the other man took the handles. That's how we got the concrete up the ramp to the top to pour it," said Elliott.

One thing Mykrantz didn't fully reckon with, when he embarked on his project, was the City of San Diego's jealousy over water rights. They took the position that water from any watercourse ultimately feeding the San Diego River was theirs. Mr. Mykrantz was duly informed that his dam was illegal and had to go. This naturally did not set too well with him. What the city didn't reckon with, however, was that besides being a water and archaeology devotee, Mykrantz was also a pretty fair city, turned country lawyer. He had no intentions of tearing down his dam.

On Nov. 26, 1923, the city filed action to contest Mykrantz' right to store water. After extensive hearings, on Jan. 29, 1925, he was issued state permit #1985 for use of 2 cubic feet per second, and 149 acre feet of storage water for 570.35 acres of irrigation and domestic use. The main dam didn't have to go completely, but the compromise did require him to lower the spillway so as not to impound more water than permitted. The result was a far cry from his original dream for the valley, but

RUINS OF THE MYKRANTZ main dam as it appears from San Vicente Road today. Another Mykrantz dam that stands today can be seen on the north side of Ramona Oaks Road.

a victory of sorts.

As it turned out, unfortunately, the whole issue became academic. Two years later, San Diego County experienced rains during the winter of 1926-27 that not only washed out his dams, but completely destroyed the family homestead, as well. From February 13th to 17th, 1927, six and one-half inches of rain fell in the City of San Diego, while the Cuyamaca Mountains received 28 inches during the same period. Train service by the Santa Fe and the San Diego & Eastern Railroads was suspended for six days, and mail had to come in by U.S. Naval boats.

After a week of incessant rain, John Mykrantz found his cellar full of water and evacuated the family, who took refuge on higher ground in the cow barns. The family, the housekeeper, the parrot and the Persian cat shared quarters in the barns with the ranch foreman, his family and milkers. At 7 pm on February 22nd, the Mykrantz' house washed down the creek.

"You could hear the nails pulling out of boards of the house just before it went downstream," June recalled. "Everything was lost. My father wouldn't let anybody go back to save their personal belongings. He said it just wasn't worth risking a life for."

Two hours after their house went down San Vicente Creek, the Mykrantzes heard frogs croaking outside. They looked out at a clear, star-filled sky. The rain had finally stopped.

That five-bedroom home, which Mykrantz had built in 1922, was situated in a small grove of live oaks just northwest of the corner of Vista Vicente Drive and

Vista Vicente Way, near the present-day 15th green of the golf course. The rampaging San Vicente Creek, like the proverbial elephant, simply sat where it wanted to, cutting a new course and taking out oaks and all in the process.

Weeks later, the contents of the home were still being picked up miles downstream in the vicinity of Lakeside.

During the depression of the 1930s, Mykrantz' San Vicente holdings diminished by 2,000 acres. He was forced to allow the more rocky and steep parts to go back to the state for delinquent taxes.

John Mykrantz died in 1943 and his wife, Elizabeth, continued to operate the ranch with the help of Dorace and June Scarbery. The Scarberys bought the ranch in 1938 and kept it going until February 1955, when they sold the major portion of their holdings to Bill Patch.

Bill Patch was a real estate developer and promoter who was active in commercial properties all around Southern California, and he was taken with backcountry real estate, as well.

The form of sale from the Scarberys was a lease and option to buy, which was drafted by Patch. This transaction eventually resulted in long and bitter litigation. The dispute revolved around the timeliness of the lease payments, and whether this constituted default. It went to the court of appeals and has since become a real estate case study for law schools. Patch's position was sustained.

The Bill Patch Land & Water Company filed a few subdivision plats and drilled several water wells. He conducted an energetic sales campaign around 1959, offering one- and two-acre sites located south of the present Rio Verde Drive and west of Rainbird Road for $2,500 to $4,500 each. He flew his own airplane and put in a landing strip that once abutted the old Sympson orange orchard just north of the present-day Rancho Barona Road.

He also sold larger parcels on Barona Mesa, touting the abundance of available water. These parcels were sold along with certain water rights to his wells in the valley and to a pipeline he ran from them up to the mesa.

Patch's water wells were drilled before the use of today's high speed rigs, which are capable of drilling through thick granite rock. His wells went down about 90 to 100 feet and were good producers during good years. Time proved, however, that during an extended drought, the length of time required for recharging the water level seriously limited their sustained production. By contrast, the wells drilled on the golf course, during the 1970s, go down 300 to 500 feet into deep aquifers and have proved to be good producers during good years and bad.

Patch had hopes of developing the whole valley into estate homesites. Plans for a golf course were drawn up, but it would be another 14 years, and two owners later, before a golf course became a reality in San Vicente.

Bill Patch's health failed and he died in 1961 before completing his project. His land and water company went into bankruptcy shortly thereafter.

The Scarberys, however, remained in San Vicente Valley long after their adversary left. June and Dorace

THE MYKRANTZ HOME, shown in 1925. It was lost during the flood of 1927.

continued to live on one of their parcels in the middle of the main valley. Dorace kept up breeding and raising prize-winning Polled Hereford cattle and palomino horses, leasing grazing land from the subsequent owners of the main ranch.

They were living in this ranch house, located off the north end of the present Scarbery Way, in 1970 when we started planning for the development of San Diego Country Estates (SDCE). They later moved to acreage they owned in the west end of the valley, the site of where the old Yorba ranch house was once located. They had to give up raising livestock when Dorace was no longer physically able to keep up with the hard work.

THE SCARBERYS, Dorace and June, are shown holding an Indian olla that they found in San Vicente Valley many years ago. Such ollas were used by the Diegueños to bury ashes of their cremated dead.

The Scarbery's last move was to a modern ranch- style home on Daza Drive, making them citizens of SDCE. They said they had to close their eyes to remember where certain things were located before their valley was filled up with streets and homes.

Other Corners
of San Vicente

BESIDES THE TWO LARGE LAND AREAS covered by San Diego Country Estates and the Barona Reservation, several other parts of the old Rancho San Vicente have seen significant settlements emerge over the past 50 years. But the largest land holding within the rancho's boundaries has remained largely undeveloped.

Monte Vista Ranch

The biggest part of the San Vicente still held in one ownership, and undeveloped, is the beautiful Monte Vista Ranch. It consists of 4,200 acres and takes in nearly all the land within the old rancho boundary lying west of Barona and south of San Vicente Road. When we came here in 1970, it was owned by W. R. Hawn of Dallas and Harry L. Summers of San Diego, who developed Rancho Bernardo during the 1960s. They had acquired the Monte Vista in 1959, when it was known as the Mirasol Ranch, from D.J. Sass and Harry Farb.

Much of this property is the same land that Thomas J. Daley bought in 1885, calling it his Barona Ranch.

Known for its 'Daley Mine,' it was the site of early copper exploration, high expectations and disappointment during the early 20th century. (See Chapter 10.)

In later days, old-timers referred to the land as the "Goat Ranch" — a name that goes back to the early 1920s when an attempt was made to raise Angora goats for their valuable wool. But that venture also failed because the animals kept getting into rough chaparral, which destroyed much of their coats.

Summers and Hawn ran cattle on the land and had success raising wine grapes and avocados. They annexed the land into the Ramona Municipal Water District during the 1960s in anticipation of future growth. They expected parts of it would eventually be ready for significant development, but that was not to happen.

By 1996 Hawn and Summers sold the entire holding to Crail Capital and Eric Johnson of Los Angeles County, whose long-range plan was to design and develop an upscale rural estate community. Their plan was dropped, however, after it met with hefty local opposition. Crail Capital sold the land in 2007 to The Nature Conservancy, who held it until the California Department of Fish and Game (CDFG) was able to buy it with State Proposition 84 bond funds and Federal Section 6 funds, intended to preserve natural resources and endangered species. The CDFG's plan is to keep it as an open space preserve.

Thus far the Monte Vista Ranch is closed and off limits to the public. Unlike the Barnett Ranch, which was acquired with county funds and has been opened to hiking and horse trails, no uses for the taxpayers are as yet planned for this lovely 4.200-acre public resource.

THE ENTRANCE TO LITTLE KLONDIKE, otherwise known as Rancho San Vicente. This settlement is located just north of the Barona Indian Reservation, on Wildcat Canyon Road.

Little Klondike

The development originally known as Little Klondike is located on the western side of Wildcat Canyon Road, just south of San Vicente Road before entering the Barona Indian Reservation. It was originally named after the Little Klondike Creek running adjacent to it. The Klondike term comes from the river where the gold rush of 1898 occurred in the Yukon Territory and because gold panning was taking place here at the time. The road into the neighborhood bares the sign "Rancho San Vicente," having been renamed by subsequent residents.

The settlement had its beginning about 1957 when the owners of the land, Sass and Farb, cut out about 100 acres from their vast Monte Vista holding. They filed a 'record of survey map' for 80 one-acre lots. That action was taken before there was a county ordinance requiring minimum improvements for new subdivisions. No paved roads, water, sanitation, electric or telephone facilities were installed. The buyer paid his money and got land — mainly land, that's it.

One of those pioneer settlers was Frederic Yockim, who bought a lot and later built a cabin retreat in 1960. It took seven years of living with a generator before Fred and his neighbor, Joe Smith, put up the money to bring in a San Diego Gas & Electric power line. Today there are about 70 residences in Little Klondike.

Rancho San Vicente

Rancho San Vicente is part of another large land holding that was undeveloped until 1998. Located in the northwest corner of the San Vicente Valley, it is bisected by Vista Ramona Road, north of Spangler Peak Drive.

Known by many as Ryland Homes, this beautiful planned community consists of 241 single-family residences on one-half to two-acre lots.

The original old ranch, which we first saw when we came here in 1970, was renowned for its stately house, its barns, and rows of eucalyptus and olive trees. It was built by Augustus Barnett for his daughter, Ellen, during the 1890s, but it was torn down in the late 1980s to make way for residential development. The adobe design of the house was similar to the home that Barnett built for his own use, which still stands today.

The ranch covered about 400 acres and has been known by many names since Augustus sold it. Many

ENTRANCE TO RANCHO SAN VICENTE, a beautiful planned community in the northwest corner of the valley, which is known to many as Ryland Homes.

old-timers referred to it as the Vanoni place for Julius Vanoni, who owned and farmed it from 1912 to 1917. John Mykrantz bought it in 1922 and sold it in 1935 to Ward and Ruby Winchel.

Others who have ranched there include Burton B. Bassett, who raised feeder calves for veal from 1935 until 1956. He usually had 300 to 350 calves that, according to Ramona historian Guy Woodward, he left on the cows until they reached 400 hundred pounds and were ready for market — a method of raising veal that is no longer economical.

George Humiston of Los Angeles acquired the ranch in 1956 and owned it for 25 years, raising cattle and hay.

The Humiston Ranch also included the 700 acres on the valley's western ridge, just outside of the rancho boundary. During the mid-1970s, Humiston leased his range land to Casey Tibbs, who ran cattle there. Several early San Diego Country Estates (SDCE) settlers have vivid memories of Casey's stock getting loose and trampling their new gardens and landscape. Casey, a former world champion rodeo cowboy, helped SDCE developer Ray Watt promote his new community. In spite of some of those problems, the neighbors still have fond memories of that cowboy.

Humiston sold the entire 1,100 acres in 1980. The part on the ridge that included much of Spangler Peak was later developed into an avocado grove. The lower part is now the beautiful Rancho San Vicente neighborhood.

Barona Mesa

Several hundred feet above, and south of Ramona Oaks, lays a large plateau that falls off to the east into the Cleveland National Forest and the San Diego River basin. Known as Barona Mesa, it was referred to by old-timers as "Cow Valley." It boasted a beautiful 30-acre orange grove and a small airstrip when we first saw it.

John Mykrantz acquired most of the mesa during the early 1920s by assembling several different ownerships. He was interested in acquiring the water rights that came with the land.

Subsequent owners of the major part of it included Dorace and June Scarbery, Bill Patch Land and Water Company, C. H. Randell, Claude Sympson, Richard Dwyer and Kishor Doshi.

THE REASON WHY Wildcat Canyon Road bears the name it has is shown here. This mountain lion was shot in 1940 near that road by Lupo Grosse, who was a long-time Ramona resident.

Bill Patch drilled wells in the valley floor, near Ramona Oaks, ran a pipeline up to the mesa, and sold land with water rights to the wells and the pipeline during the 1950s. His first taker was C. H. Randell, who established a nursery that evolved into a beautiful 30-acre orange and avocado orchard. The grove was owned by Claude Sympson of Santa Ana for more than 25 years.

At the time SDCE started developing, Richard Dwyer, a Los Angeles mortgage broker, owned the 550-plus acres that fell adjacent to the grove. He planted more than 4,500 eucalyptus trees in the late 1970s in anticipation of developing four-acre parcels. Only a fraction of those trees have survived over the years since.

In 1982, Kishor Doshi acquired 300 acres of that land, calling it Barona Mesa Estates and developed it into 62 four-plus acre home sites with two and a half miles of paved roads and electrical/telephone utilities. Beautiful estate homes have been built by the parcel owners, who put in their own water wells and septic systems.

Further development has taken place in recent years, just south of Barona Mesa Estates and outside the rancho boundary. Four Corners Estates contains 30 to 35 homes developed, for the most part, on unpaved roads. It occupies an area that has been known for many years as Four Corners. It was owned and occupied during the 1970s and 1980s by Pat Peil, who operated a motorcycle race course and decomposed granite borrow pit from time to time.

Creekside

The small neighborhood of Creekside is located along San Vicente Creek east of Wildcat Canyon Road and across from Little Klondike. Part of the old Barnett Ranch, it was acquired by Watt in 1971, along with land north of San Vicente Road, to facilitate his wastewater treatment and water reclamation program.

Today Creekside, consisting of around 100 acres, is home to about 40 estate residences along Tombill Road. The history of the land is all about Augustus Barnett, as told, starting on page 109.

The story of how the 'Tombill Road' name came about is another tale. It comes from the names 'Tom' and 'Bill,' who planted most of those eucalyptus trees that line the road, who worked in the small vineyard above it, and are sons of the author, who owned part of that acreage.

It was later subdivided for residential development during the 1990s into two-acre parcels by Luke Parker, Brian Coble and Ruth Friery.

Ramona Oaks

THE LOVELY OAK-SHADED GLEN, with the old farmhouses, its picnic grounds and the pool that we know today as Ramona Oaks Park, had its beginnings about 1919. That's when Harry Weiss acquired the approximately 960 acres that takes in the eastern end of San Vicente Valley. When Weiss owned it, he called it Oak Knoll Ranch.

Weiss, a wealthy Los Angeleno whose family made their fortune from Pennsylvania soft coal, needed a place to breed and keep his polo ponies. He and his son, Reggie, were prominent in the Coronado polo set.

The main farmhouse, with its comfortable bungalow design, and the guest house next to it, were built by Weiss in 1920 and stand today very much as they did when first built. In fact, the 'Weiss house' now serves as the headquarters for the San Diego Country Estates Recreation Department. However, a big red barn across the creek from the present picnic grounds, which stood until the mid-1980s, was not built until 1930. The barn construction happened well after Weiss sold the ranch to Dave Dyas, who did build it — and a long, long time after the Butterfield Stage ceased operations in 1861.

What does the Butterfield Stage have to do with Ramona Oaks, you ask? Nothing, of course, but enough people thought it did that a feature article appeared in a 1980 edition of the San Diego Tribune, showing a picture of the barn with a caption stating that it once was a Butterfield Stage station. The perpetrators of that yarn were off more than just a little. The closest the stage ever came to San Vicente was Warner's Ranch, some 30 miles away, and that happened 70 years before the barn was built.

In January 1926, Harry Weiss sold the ranch to David S. Dyas, a motion picture actor. Dyas was suffering from tuberculosis, and his parents and brother, B. J. Dyas, owner of a Hollywood department store, helped him buy it as a retreat for his health. The famous movie character actor Wallace Berry was a good friend of Dyas and a frequent visitor at the ranch during that time. The Dyas family sold the ranch after David died in 1933.

Through the 1930s, '40s, and '50s, Ramona Oaks knew several owners, including James R. Armstrong, Mrs. Ethel Phillips, C. Melvin McCuen and the Anglo Aryan Foundation.

In 1955, the property was purchased by the Action Stamp Company of San Diego for use as a promotional attraction. They were in the trading stamp business and one of the premiums offered was the use of the picnic grounds and camping facilities at Ramona Oaks Park. So many stamps redeemed would buy a day of picnicking under the oaks and swimming in the pool that was built into the

RAMONA OAKS IN 1958. This pool was built into the San Vicente Creek, a part of the Action Ranch resort facility. Ruins of the pool are still in evidence today.

creek. So many more stamps entitled one to camp there over the weekend. The pool in the creek was subsequently replaced with the junior Olympic pool in use today, but remains of the old creek pool are still in evidence.

In 1959, Action leased the property to Lew Drago and Chuck Apgar, who operated the resort facility until 1962, when it was sold to Union Oil Company of California.

It was while Union Oil owned it that the San Diego County Sheriff's Association became involved with the operation and maintenance of Ramona Oaks. It seems the Sheriff's Department was called upon to break up one of the first big pot-party love-ins that attracted national media attention during the 1960s.

The deputies convinced Union Oil they could do a better job of caretaking the place than those who had been in charge. The deputy's association offered to provide maintenance and care of the property in return for its use as a training and recreation facility for members and their families.

When we came to the valley in 1970, Deputy Jack Everett and his family were living in the old Weiss farmhouse as full-time caretakers. Jack later was killed there when the horse he was riding at full gallop, in pursuit of a calf, tripped in a gopher hole and violently threw him to the ground. Everett Place in San Diego Country Estates (SDCE) was named for Jack and his family.

In planning SDCE, we recognized the unique value Ramona Oaks represented as a community facility. Rather than subdividing it, it was set aside as a permanent park for SDCE property owners.

Before the permanent Western equestrian center was built, the old barn at Ramona Oaks served as the center for the rent-string horse operation. Marshall Cope and his wife, Denise, operated this facility, and many early lot purchasers have fond memories of the trail rides in those days before Unit VI had streets. Cope Road was named for Marshall and Denise.

A Community Designed for Living

AS THE DECADE of the 1960s was winding down, Raymond A. Watt was looking at literally dozens of large land holdings in the fast growing San Diego County. He had in mind perhaps someday developing a unique new community in that part of the country.

He had sold his successful R. A. Watt Building Company to a large conglomerate corporation in 1966. His reputation was firmly established as one of the most innovative builders and developers in the nation. Watt's activities had been centered primarily in the Los Angeles area, where he developed housing, industrial and commercial projects that won him national awards and worldwide recognition.

Watt stayed on with the new corporation as chief operating officer, running his old organization. However, when Richard Nixon was elected president in 1968, Watt left to accept a presidential appointment with the new administration in Washington. He served as a close adviser to George Romney, who was secretary of housing and urban development.

After a year at this post, the itch to get back into the private sector became just too strong. Watt resigned that full-time assignment, but agreed to take on a less time-consuming appointment for the President. He became the first president of the newly formed National Housing Partnership Corporation, a private/public sector consortium created by Congress to stimulate the creation of affordable housing in the nation.

These public service contributions were not the only ones Watt was to make over the years. During the Ford and Carter administrations, he served as a member of the Federal Home Loan Bank Board. He also had a long-standing relationship with the University of Southern California as a prominent member of its board of trustees.

Watt's first major venture after returning to the private sector proved to be perhaps the most demanding and financially challenging of his long career. It involved the planning, governmental processing, financing, construction and marketing of a totally new community — San Diego Country Estates (SDCE).

Watt closed the purchase of 3,250 acres in the San Vicente Valley on New Year's Eve of 1969. The acquisition consisted of two major parcels. One was 2,650 acres in the central and westerly part of the valley, which was owned by a syndicate from Long Beach headed by Charles Hughes. The other was owned by Union Oil Company of California and took in 600 acres of the eastern part of the valley. Two long-time associates of Watt's, real estate broker Rod Johanson and attorney Phillip Nicholson, were instrumental in locating the property and negotiating the sale.

I was working for Governor Reagan as state director of housing and community development when I first met Ray Watt in 1967. In that position I had the pleasure of working with some of the top builders, developers, and real estate and lending institution leaders in the country. Being a businessman, I intended to spend but one term in the Reagan administration and go back to the private sector after three to four years of full-time public service.

When Watt learned of my plans in April, 1970, he asked if I would care to look at a large tract of land he had recently bought in San Diego County and see what I thought of it. I was naturally intrigued. First of all, the prospect of possibly being associated with a developer with his fine reputation presented a rare opportunity. Secondly, while in government service, I had developed a deep interest in planned communities and new towns.

After seeing San Vicente Valley, I was sold. We formed an association in July 1970 that lasted for many years and contributed to several other successful developments, not the least of which is Fairbanks Ranch in Rancho Santa Fe, California.

The Development Plan

The objective of San Diego Country Estates was to create a low-density, environmentally sensitive residential community that would appeal to a mixed market of primary and secondary homeowners. The healthful climate and beautiful views would be fully exploited. Amenities would include an extensive amount of common space (1,300 acres, which is 42% of the entire tract), and recreational improvements, including a first-class golf course, equestrian, tennis and park facilities.

Mass grading for house pads would not be allowed, and streets and building sites would be designed to follow the natural contours of the land. Lots, complete with all public services, would be sold to owners who would design and build their own homes. All utilities would be underground. A fire station, three school sites, and a commercial center would also be provided. Overall residential density would approximate one dwelling unit per acre. Of the total of 3,444 dwelling units approved for development, fewer than 400 would be condominiums.

Using these concepts, a land-use plan was developed by the engineering and planning firm of E.L. Pearson and Associates. Don Davis and Fred Youngdahl were Pearson's project engineers assigned to the job. The plan was ready to submit to the County of San Diego for approval by September 1970. It was the first such plan to be processed under a new county policy requiring that detailed, specific plans be submitted for approval for large-scale projects.

In earlier days, the process of subdividing land was much simpler: acquire a tract of land, file a plot for its layout into blocks and lots or parcels, and when that was accomplished, look for willing buyers. This course of action was followed by the San Francisco syndicate in the 1870s, Daley in the 1880s and Patch, Sass and Farb in the 1950s. All that those early speculators had to contend with was financing and the fickle turns of the

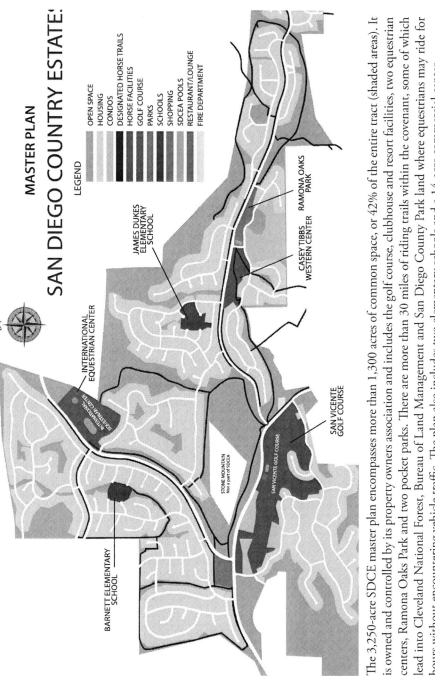

The 3,250-acre SDCE master plan encompasses more than 1,300 acres of common space, or 42% of the entire tract (shaded areas). It is owned and controlled by its property owners association and includes the golf course, clubhouse and resort facilities, two equestrian centers, Ramona Oaks Park and two pocket parks. There are more than 30 miles of riding trails within the covenant, some of which lead into Cleveland National Forest, Bureau of Land Management and San Diego County Park land where equestrians may ride for hours without encountering vehicle traffic. The plan also includes two elementary schools and a 14-acre commercial center.

economy (which are awesome enough). The development and sale of land in California since the late 1960s has been a much more complex proposition altogether.

Before the governmental approval process was finally completed for San Diego Country Estates, there would be more than 70 advertised public hearings. These steps included approvals of a private development plan, a specific plan, a general plan change, five tentative and final subdivision maps, and many special use permits. Each condominium phase required use permits, and tentative and final maps, while each recreational facility also needed a special use permit. All these steps required public hearings before the planning commission and, in some cases, the county board of supervisors.

Providing water and fire services for the new community called for annexations to the existing Ramona districts. A new sanitation district also had to be formed within the Ramona Municipal Water District. These additions required proceedings before the appropriate district's board of directors, as well as the county's Local Agency Formation Commission. In the case of the new sanitation district, it was necessary to have a public hearing before the State Regional Water Quality Control Board to establish discharge standards for the wastewater treatment plant.

The sheer number of formal and informal actions required for governmental approval of the development is impressive enough. What is even more noteworthy is that with all those opportunities for public input, there was only one person who registered a formal protest at these public hearings. That was a neighboring landowner who

LARGE EARTH MOVERS grade lower Vista Vicente Road near Calistoga Drive in 1973.

SDCE'S FIRST CONDOMINIUMS are under construction in June 1973. Seen in the background is the 13th hole on the San Vicente Golf Course, with its newly planted eucalyptus trees.

felt that the location originally planned for the wastewater treatment plant was too close to his property. As a result, Watt found a different site and built the plant there.

Throughout this long and involved process, there were several government officials who stood out as friends of the proposed plan and without their help, this community would not be what it is today. Among the elected officials was William "Bill" Craven, who was county supervisor for this district at the time the crucial votes were cast. Bill went on to distinguish himself as a California state assemblyman and senator. Among his many achievements as a legislator was leading the establishment of California State University at San Marcos. Other governmental officials who were most helpful included Dan Cherrier, county planning director; Garry Butterfield, general manager of the Ramona Municipal Water District, and Bill Hannigan, chairman of the Ramona Fire Protection District.

Building and
Selling SDCE

IT WASN'T UNTIL EARLY 1972 that enough governmental approvals were obtained to allow developer Ray Watt to proceed with capital improvements for San Diego Country Estates (SDCE). About this time Ray's brother, Bill Watt, joined the effort as co-developer and became active in managing the project.

Golf Course Design and Construction

The first major improvement to be started was the golf course. Fred Harris had been hired about a year earlier to be golf course superintendent and was waiting with strained patience for the go-ahead on construction. However, during that year, time had not been wasted. Plans were prepared by golf course architect Ted Robinson, and contractors were selected. The design concept was to use the natural attributes of the flood plain and abutting land. Few, if any, live oaks were to be removed. Liberal latitude was given to allow for an imaginative and challenging course, rather than to force its design to conform to a rigid subdivision plan. That concept produced a layout

GRAND OPENING of the San Vicente Country Estates Clubhouse in October 1972. Shown (from left) are SDCE codeveloper Bill Watt, Lillian Dianne Wagner, SDCE executive vice president Chuck LeMenager, SDCE developer Ray Watt, Mimi Craven, San Diego County Supervisor Bill Craven and SDCE marketing director Donal MacAdam.

considered to be one of the best in the county.

The course was constructed and ready for business in record time. The first official round was played in February 1973, almost one year to the day after construction began. Three local contractors who played a big role in the effort were Dale Carrol of Ballena, Art Thomsen of Ramona and Milt Angel of Mesa Grande. Dale was responsible for building the greens and tees. Milt and Art did all the heavy and finish earth moving. As a tribute to Ted

Robinson's design skill, less than 200,000 cubic yards of earth were moved and, only seven oaks eliminated. The name San Vicente Golf Course was not the only one considered. Serious thought was given to naming it Ramona Oaks Golf Course, and even the name Wildcat Canyon Golf Course was considered. But the natural name is the one that won out in the end. Ray Watt's concept of development was to put in as much of the planned amenities as possible, up front. He wanted potential buyers to see what they were getting, rather than having to visualize it. The golf course, first equestrian center and clubhouse facilities were finished, or nearly so, when lot sales began in October 1972.

Equestrian Emphasis

At that time, the International Equestrian Center (IEC) was functional and ready for its first major event. It was the "California Championship Grand Prix," held in November 1972, and it was our first chance to show off our commitment to horses. It attracted hundreds of spectators who drove out on then unpaved roads to see 40 top competitors in the sport and take a look at the valley.

Providing for the needs of horses and equestrian facilities was a significant factor in the plan we fashioned back in 1970. Donal MacAdam, marketing director, and member of the planning team, was a strong advocate for making this a 'horse community.' Studies had shown that San Diego County was one of the most heavily horse-populated counties in the U.S., and Watt was convinced we had a good opportunity to capitalize on this potential market. Instead of building just one fine equestrian facility,

THE INTERNATIONAL EQUESTRIAN CENTER held its first grand prix in November 1972, shortly after it opened, before there were streets or homes built in the area.

he built two — one to serve the hunter-jumper, saddlebred and show horse folks (the IEC), and another for the Western, rodeo and trail riders. The 'Western Center' was later renamed in honor of rodeo cowboy Casey Tibbs, who

PONY CLUB COMPETITION. Rachael Jones performs on the jumper course at the International Equestrian Center during a 1989 show.

moved to the estates in 1973 and lived there until his death in 1990. Miles upon miles of horse trails were also planned for our 1,300 acres of common area.

A second major horse show, held just nine months later, was even bigger. It was a six-day Grand Prix in June 1973, and it attracted 130 horses competing for nearly $100,000 in prizes. The entry list read like a roll call of champions, and the judges included Neal Shapiro, one of the U.S. Olympic equestrian team's highest medalist. All spectator admission fees for the last two days of the show were donated to the City of Hope.

Casey Tibbs Western Center

The Western facility also had its share of memorable promotions about that time. They included an "all-girl rodeo," a bronc riding clinic, and the housing of youth tennis campers in the new unoccupied stables.

Our first major event at the new center was the 1973 Western States All-Girl Rodeo, held in February. The barns weren't finished yet, but the rodeo ring and spectator stands were in place. It rained steadily the day before and during the event, but that didn't seem to dampen the spirits of the young contestants, nor of the crowd of 2,000. Women rode broncs, roped calves, tied goats and got into team roping. Winners of cash prizes came from as far away as Northern California, Las Vegas and Texas.

The tennis campers who were put up in horse stalls were attending one-week camps in the summer of 1974, which were being held across Pappas Road at our new tennis ranch that was about to open. The camp was run by Myron McNamara, coach of UC Irvine's champion tennis team at the time. Bunks were placed in the stalls, not as yet occupied by their intended equine tenants, and temporary showers and toilets were built where the horse wash racks were to go. The kids were bused down to the new golf club restaurant for their meals three times a day. The camp was challenging enough, with Myron's driving teaching style, but a hotter than usual summer, with many days of 103-plus degree temperatures, made it tougher. To many of those kids, from mostly affluent families, the accommodations seemed more like a boot camp than a summer tennis resort.

Casey Tibbs had joined the developer's team to help

CASEY TIBBS with a miniature replica of a bronze statue of himself riding the famous bronc "Necktie." The original, which was erected at the ProRodeo Hall of Fame in Colorado Springs, is one-and-a-half times larger than life-size of the former world champion bronc rider.

THE RAMONA SANTANA RIDERS enjoyed the last gymkhana show of 2012 at the Casey Tibbs Western Center.

THIS TEAM CALF ROPING participant doesn't let the mud bother her during the 1973 Western States All-Girl Rodeo held at the Western Center.

BARREL RACING is always a highlight at a gymkhana show. Kara Zulkoski is shown cutting a tight turn at the Casey Tibbs Western Center in 1990.

promote Western activities. A world champion bronc rider several times, and a member of the ProRodeo Hall of Fame, he was widely popular among rodeo folk. His picture had once graced the cover of Life Magazine. Even Roy Rogers came here to be his best man when he was married in Ramona Oaks Park.

Tibbs came up with the idea of putting on a bronc riding clinic. In response to his many young admirers nationally, he scheduled a couple of one-week camps at the Western Center. Among these aspirants was none other than Steve Ford, son of then sitting president of the United States, Gerald Ford. Naturally, Steve's presence caused quite a stir around these parts. It was some sight watching the president's son dragging himself back up out of the dust, only to be violently thrown back down off the bucking machine. All the while Secret Service men, hired to protect this dignitary, simply stood and watched. Their vigil was apparently focused more on kidnappers and assassins than the potentially lethal effects of that machine.

Environmental Quality Advisory Board

During the early stages of construction, Watt established an environmental quality advisory board to help carry out our developmental goals. This panel of experts met monthly to review project plans and progress. Their suggestions and advice played an important part in enhancing the livability of SDCE.

The board was comprised of Harvey O. Banks, noted water expert and former California Director of Water Resources; E. Robert Bichowsky, local agribusiness man and member of the University of California's Agricultural

Advisory Board; Dr. Harry N. Coulombe, director of the Bureau of Ecology at California State University at San Diego; Dr. James R. Moriarty, professor of history and anthropology at the University of San Diego; Dr. Richard B. Tibby, professor of biology, University of Southern California, and the author, former California Director of Housing and Community Development.

Infrastructure Improvements

Between September 1972, when the first improvement plans were signed by the county, and April 1978, when work on the last phase of the development was done, Watt spent more than $21 million on public works facilities alone. Inflation during that era would have caused that price tag to double, had he bid out the work only five years later.

Public works are the type of improvements that are not highly visible, but without them, a community cannot exist today. They include water distribution, sewers and wastewater treatment, storm drains and flood control structures, underground electric, telephone and TV cables, and, of course, paved streets and streetlights.

To get water to every home in the estates required building four miles of 14- and 12-inch water main down San Vicente Road from Hansen Lane to the pump station near Arena Drive. Four reservoirs, with six million gallons of storage capacity, were provided. From these reservoirs, water is distributed to every lot through a total of 46 miles of 6- to 10-inch water lines.

Sewage and wastewater is collected by 52 miles of 8- to 18-inch lines, ending at the wastewater treatment

EFFECTS OF THE 1980 WINTER FLOOD. The 18th green (now the 9th green) is shown after a 50-year intensity flood roared down San Vicente Creek. As a result, parts of the golf course were redesigned and riprap was installed under the turf in more vulnerable areas. All home lots were sited outside of the flood plain and were unaffected.

and water reclamation plant. As a condition of county approval for SDCE's master plan, treated effluent from the plant was to be used for irrigating the golf course. The discharge standards set for this $1.5 million facility are so high that some water leaving it is actually as good as the tap water supplied in many cities. Neste, Brudin and Stone, the engineering firm that designed the system, won the 'Award of the Year' from the San Diego Chapter of American Civil Engineering Association for the design.

More than seven miles of storm drain pipes, from 18 to 84 inches in diameter, cross various roadways in the development. Compounding the problem for the designers was the fact that the system not only has to handle runoff from SDCE's own 3,250 acres, but from an additional area totaling 5,000 acres that drains into the valley. These facilities were designed to handle the volume of runoff that would result from the worst storm likely to occur in 100 years. We didn't want any homes in our development to meet the same fate as John Mykrantz did in 1927 when his house was washed down into San Vicente Creek.

To meet these stringent requirements, a 10-foot high by 60-foot long reinforced concrete box culvert was installed beneath Vista Vicente Drive where it crosses San Vicente Creek. And 20 more large reinforced concrete culverts were built in other areas of the estates.

The 43 miles of paved roads constructed in the estates represent a great compromise between engineering needs, practicality and environmental concerns. On several occasions, a road was redesigned and diverted in order to save an ancient oak tree.

The man who was responsible for supervising the design and construction of all these public works, and did such a fine job of it, was Constantine "Gus" Pappas.

On-site construction, such as the building of the clubhouses, condominiums, commercial facilities and the like, was under the able direction of long-time Watt associate Phillip Overton. Architectural design for the clubhouse, lodge, rotunda at the IEC, model homes for Bill Watt on Watt Road and the Bobby Riggs house on the first fairway was done by Lee F. Wilcox & Associates, AIA.

Backcountry Fires

As plans for San Diego Country Estates were being developed, one of San Diego County's most devastating fires struck the Laguna Mountains in September 1970.

It was the biggest in the county's recorded history and the state's largest since the 1930s.

Nearly 175,000 acres were burning and ash from the fire was raining in downtown San Diego. As it happened, we were actually discussing our development plans at the county's planning department, then located on Harbor Drive. It reminded all of us that Mother Nature periodically clears old native growth, with unexpected fury. Consequently, our subdivision and improvement plans were drawn giving careful study to fire prevention and suppression for backcountry development.

With San Vicente Road essentially one long cul-de-sac, it was clear that the valley needed a new secondary road for better access. Accordingly, we bought right-of-way from seven different landowners and paid for the construction of the two-lane Vista Ramona Road, which runs from SDCE's northwest corner to join the Old Julian Highway, to provide that added access.

Four water storage tanks, holding a total of six million gallons, were built in strategic locations to back up fire flow needs for the many hydrants installed. A new fire station was built and conveyed to the Ramona Fire Protection District.

These improvements served the community well in later years when, on three different occasions, the valley was hit by devastating major fires.

Indian Head Fire

On Mother's Day in May 1972, while infrastructure was under construction, a massive burn swept in from the Barona Reservation over Indian Head Hill. It covered the future neighborhoods around Barona Mesa Road and Calistoga Place. Aerial tankers dropped retardant on chaparral-covered slopes, turning orange some areas that were soon to be planted for green golf course turf.

The fire lasted several days, with Ramona Oaks Park serving as the staging area and campground for firefighting crews. No homes or other structures had yet been built in the area so there were minimal improvement losses. But the normally beautiful vista we saw from the clubhouse site was left with charred chaparral and scorched rocks. It was not a very encouraging scene for the sales force gearing up for a grand sales opening due to start in two months.

Cedar Fire

But SDCE would not be so lucky the next time. On October 25, 2003, the devastating Cedar Fire swept into the peaceful east end of SDCE from the San Diego River Basin. It had started in the Julian area of Pine Hills, and from 5:37 pm, when first reported, until midnight, it burned 5,000 acres. Pushed by winds of 40 and 50 mph, it quickly devoured four homes on Cherish Way and Love Lane. Between midnight and dawn, it leaped westward from one neighborhood to another, burning over some open space corridors and licking at homes and yards. Before it was finally extinguished, 25 homes in the estates were totally destroyed, eight were damaged and three barns were lost at the International Equestrian Center.

Exiting the estates, the firestorm continued to the west and south, raging down Wildcat Canyon Road, consuming eight homes in Little Klondike and going on into the Barona Reservation, down Mussey Grade Road and west to Poway and Scripps Ranch. The residential losses in SDCE, while tragic, amounted to less than one percent of the total of 3,332 houses there.

The devastation in some of those other communities was much worst. The Barona Tribe lost 39 homes, a preschool and more than 2,000 acres of hillside chaparral. The San Diego City suburb of Scripps Ranch had losses five to six times greater than SDCE, with 340 homes destroyed out of 7,000, or almost five percent of that community.

It was the worst wildfire in San Diego County since the Laguna Fire. The Cedar Fire killed 15 people, destroyed 2,232 homes and burned 280,000 acres (438 square miles).

Witch Creek Fire

Four years later, again during the month of October, this time on the 21st of 2007, we were suddenly shaken by yet another wildfire. Starting in the Witch Creek area near Ballena, it swept west, consuming more than 160,000 acres before it was eventually contained in Rancho Bernardo.

It generally followed the Old Julian Highway, going into northern areas of Ramona, where it destroyed 400 residential and non-residential structures and moved on to the southern ridges above San Pasqual Valley. Before it was finished, the inferno had burned its way through the northern sector of Ramona, all the way into Rancho Bernardo, where it destroyed 360 homes.

Prevailing winds kept it from lapping too far down into the San Vicente Valley, but it did not totally spare SDCE.

The fire itself did relatively little structural damage in SDCE, but backyards on the lower western slope of Mount Gower along Kerri Lane and Poderio Drive were scourged, with outbuildings burned, as were others on the northern fringe of the Rancho San Vicente neighborhood. Two homes on Vista Ramona were lost.

Mandatory evacuation orders caused one of the biggest traffic jams that the Ramona area had ever seen. Hundreds of cars clogged San Vicente Road into town and onto Highway 67. A virtual breakdown in communications resulted in hundreds of people being denied re-entry to their homes for days.

Master of Marketing

While the physical aspects of SDCE will stand as an outstanding example of enlightened planning and development for years to come, the more remarkable achievement was the sale of more than 3,000 backcountry home sites in a period of five short years. Only a marketing genius like Ray Watt could have done it.

During that five-year period, the nation went through two economic crises that had profound impacts on the sales of remote properties. A third sales constraint entered the picture during the early 1970s when the California State Legislature enacted a series of laws that placed more governmental control on the development and sales of land projects in rural areas.

One was a provision that allowed potential buyers 14 days to cancel their purchase at will and without any

MASTER OF MARKETING RAY WATT (center) stands next to a lot sales status board at the SDCE sales pavilion in 1972. Also shown are co-developer Bill Watt (left) and the author.

penalty. Watt's marketing practice called for complete customer satisfaction, and buyers were encouraged to check out their sites before making a commitment. However, the net result of that law was to increase the number of sales rescissions and drastically escalate marketing costs.

Several marketing directors were in charge of the sale of SDCE property in the early years. The first, and most prominent, was Donal MacAdam, head of American Land Systems, followed by Jay Browne, James Potter, William Friery, Hank Askin, Kenneth Kilbourn and Ruth Juhl. Juhl had been associated with SDCE marketing since the beginning of the development.

Notable Sports Advisers

During this 1972-77 period, Watt conducted a constant program of promotional events aimed at attracting attention to the valley. Besides promoting the scenic and healthful environment, these events centered around golf, tennis and horses. Several renowned personalities were retained to represent SDCE's activities and facilities.

Tony Trabert, famous Davis Cup star, U.S. and Wimbledon champion, was the tennis director. While Chuck Jones served as resident pro, Al Geiberger helped promote the San Vicente Golf Course on the PGA tour and conducted golf clinics at the club.

Several fine horse people assisted in the promotion of these facilities. In addition to Casey Tibbs, the others included Jimmy Kohn, champion grand prix rider, Jack Avant, thoroughbred racehorse trainer, and Budd Boetticher, film director and trainer of Lusitano horses.

Budd and wife Mary raised and trained this special breed, which is the Portuguese version of the famous Andalusian bullfighting horses used in Spain. They built a small replica of a bullring in one of the IEC's training rings and put on free exhibitions. This attraction drew not only property owners and prospective buyers, but several notable Hollywood friends, including William Holden and John Ford, who came by to visit. Like Casey Tibbs, the Boettichers liked San Vicente so well that Bud spent the rest of his life here. He passed away in 2001.

The list of promotional events at SDCE ran the gamut. There was always something planned, it seemed, that would interest some group or another. Besides the major horse events, Watt was ever on the alert to create "excitement." The activities included fashion and vintage car shows, celebrity tennis matches featuring Charlton Heston, Elke Sommer and Ross Martin, as well as a Davis Cup tennis players' reunion, golf and tennis clinics with star players, property owners' picnics and Hawaiian luaus. One of the most memorable involved busing in the full San Diego Symphony Orchestra, who set up on the Pappas Road pavement above the picnic area in Ramona Oaks Park. The full orchestral effect of music by Dvorak, Gershwin, Copeland, Beethoven and their like resonating from the Gower Mountain boulders was truly astounding.

First Tennis Battle of the Sexes

One of those planned promotions developed into a real PR coup that was probably the single most widely viewed happening in the history of land sales promotions. Tens of millions of sports fans in eight countries around the world saw the event on television, and perhaps more than any other single thing, it helped launch the big tennis boom of the 1970s. The fact that it attracted the attention of thousands of potential lot buyers to San Diego Country Estates was not bad from Watt's standpoint either.

The idea was the brainchild of Tony Trabert and Larry Laurie. Laurie was a Los Angeles-based public relations consultant who handled Watt's press relations, and while working for another developer, had a hand in bringing the London Bridge to the desert community of Lake Havasu City, Ariz., several years earlier.

Trabert brought up the idea at a sales meeting in which different ideas were being considered for the 1973 calendar of promotional events. It seems his longtime friend Bobby Riggs had mentioned to him that he would like to show up Billy Jean King in a "battle of the sexes" tennis match. Both Riggs and King were Wimbledon and U.S. champions. Riggs, however, was 55 years old at the time, and Billy Jean was more than 30 years his junior.

King, a well-known active feminist, was constantly crusading for more recognition of professional women's tennis and decrying the lack of equality in the money paid to women. Riggs took the position that "women athletes didn't play as well as men anyway, and were lucky to get as much as they did for their inferior performances."

A press conference was called in February 1973 at the Westgate Hotel in San Diego where a luncheon was served by white-gloved waiters. Reporters from all the major wire services, as well as those from the Copley Press and the Los Angeles Times, were there. Trabert introduced Riggs, and Bobby took it from there amid lighthearted ribbing from the reporters, who all knew of his reputation for being a hustler. He gave a brief history of how the game had evolved from virtually an all-amateur sport to the play-for-pay sport it is today.

Riggs went on in this vein, as to how even the women were making big money, but Billy Jean King was still not satisfied. With that, he whipped out a cashier's check for $5,000, and issued a challenge. He, Bobby Riggs, a relatively old man, could beat the best of the women tennis players in their prime, and if he couldn't, King could have 'his' $5,000.

"Telegrams," he announced, "are being sent to King's home in Oakland, Calif., as well as to Indianapolis,"

MARGARET COURT HOLDS THE ROSES that Bobby Riggs (right) gave her for Mother's Day in 1973 just before their match. The man in the middle is CBS Television sportscaster Pat Summerall.

where King was engaged in a tournament. A deadline was set for the following Monday for her to accept the challenge. If she didn't, then the next highest ranking woman player in the world, Margaret Court, would receive the same challenge.

The match would be played "at my good friend Tony Trabert's new club — someplace called San Diego Country Estates, I think," so said Riggs.

As it developed, Billy Jean ignored him. But 10 days later, a news story came over the wire services to the effect that Margaret Court was issuing a challenge to Riggs. Only the money involved would be $10,000 and the event was to be held at the Jockey Club in Miami Beach. "My God," we thought, "someone's trying to steal our show!"

Bobby hung tough, however. He said it was his idea, and the event would be held in San Diego County or no place at all. As far as upping the stakes to ten grand — that was just fine with him. The date was set for Mother's day, May 13, 1973.

Between March 1st and the day of the event, papers all over the world carried the story about the upcoming "battle of the sexes," which was to be held in some obscure place called San Diego Country Estates in Ramona, Calif.

CBS bought the television rights. In addition to the United States, Canada, France, England, Italy, Mexico, Australia and Japan also carried the match on live television.

For a week preceding the event, reporters bedded down at SDCE's San Vicente Lodge, cranking out stories about Bobby's training program. He was on a daily diet that included some 75 vitamin and mineral tablets, and he could be seen every morning and evening jogging up and down hills and across the golf course.

These reporters came from all over: The New York Times, Sports Illustrated, the Chicago Tribune, the Los Angeles Times, and several others which escape my memory. One of these newsmen was Will Grimsley of the Associated Press, author of one of the most comprehensive books about tennis on the market at that time.

Margaret Court arrived at SDCE two days before the day of the event with her husband and year-old son. From that moment on, Bobby took every opportunity he could to try to 'psych her out.' She was, he said, "a great player but you chose the wrong coach for this match" — and so on and so on. As the final gesture, just before the match, he presented her with a dozen red roses for Mother's Day.

Sunday morning, May 13th, brought dreary weather all over Southern California. Rain was falling in most parts and dark clouds hung heavy over the San Vicente Valley.

Temporary bleachers had been set up on the north end of the court #1 and covered court #2. With the permanent stands on the east side, 5,000 people could be seated for the spectacle. (Watt donated all the proceeds from admissions to the event to the San Diego County Diabetic Association.)

By 11 a.m., when festivities were to begin, all seats were full and the television cameras, stationed on special scaffolding erected at the south end of the court, were ready. At that precise time, the "Good Lord" pushed the clouds aside and the sun shown brightly down on San Vicente for 10 million people to see. In the crowd of spectators were such notables as John Wayne, Don Budge, Jack Kramer and many other sports and show business personalities.

To many, the match seemed anticlimactic. Margaret was not in her best form, and the outcome showed it. Bobby defeated her 6-2, 6-1 in less than 45 minutes.

Almost miraculously, as the match ended and the players were shaking hands, the clouds moved back to cover the valley for the rest of the day. The world witnessed an embarrassing, but temporary, setback for the women's movement.

The total cost of the event to Watt was less than $30,000. The value of the press and television exposure was estimated at many millions of dollars, a pretty fair return on investment by anyone's standards. Bobby, who before that event, was known only to old-time tennis buffs and sports fans, had been re-propelled into instant fame. His picture appeared on the cover of Time Magazine and he was a household name throughout the nation.

In less than a year, another "battle of the sexes" was promoted by others and held in Houston, but this time Bobby played Billy Jean King. The outcome was reversed, with Bobby being beaten almost as badly as he had beaten Margaret.

The desired sales promotion results for SDCE had been realized. Throughout the summer and fall of 1973, after the match, lot sales averaged 100 to 125 per month.

It's been said those matches played a huge part in the 'Women's Movement' of the 1970s and the enactment of the Title IX federal law that banned sexual discrimination in school sports. It also helped fuel the tennis craze of that decade. New tennis camps sprung up over the nation, for kids and affluent adults alike.

Watt also recognized the demand for more facilities at San Vicente. By the summer of 1974, plans were approved and construction began on a 20-court tennis club, with clubhouse and pool. Tennis legend Rod Laver was engaged to establish one of his famous tennis camp programs, but his involvement lasted less than a year. Other programs have followed, which have helped establish the facility, now called Riviera Oaks Racquet Club, as one of the finest in San Diego County.

RIVIERA OAKS RESORT & RACQUET CLUB, with its 20 tennis courts and swimming pool, is an amenity for the enjoyment of the two adjoining time-share complexes It is also a popular center for various tennis programs, and membership is open to non-timeshare owners, as well.

Timeshare Comes to the Valley

About this time, a new phenomenon, called "time-share," was starting to sweep the vacation home industry. With county approval of 200 condominium units next to the new tennis ranch, Watt decided to devote 64 of them to that program. With assistance from Dick Thorman and Bill Friery, he decided to build a facility to attract that new market. He called it "The Good Life," and in spite of the valley's remote location, buyers found it to be one of their favorite destinations.

Watt also started something new in that industry —"the floating timeshare." Instead of holding buyers to specific 7- or 14-day periods, like most other such programs did, owners were allowed to use increments of a few days at a time throughout the year. It was another Watt innovation.

More timeshare units were added in the valley when 70 were developed in 1992 adjacent to Ramona Oaks Park by Pacific Monarch Resorts. Called "Riviera Oaks," their owner amenities were expanded when they acquired control of the trail horse operation at the Casey Tibbs Western Center and ownership of the tennis ranch. Today the two timeshare organizations share use and operation of that tennis facility.

Ups and Downs of a Great Success

The extraordinary pace of SDCE lot sales in 1973 lasted only about six months, however. It came to an abrupt slowdown with the onset of the oil crisis during the winter of 1973-74. Long lines at the fuel pumps had a dampening effect on anyone thinking about buying a building site in the backcountry.

As if that weren't bad enough, that crisis led into another, the recession of 1974-75. By that time Watt had made a considerably large financial commitment in SDCE. Lesser developers would not have survived such a set of reversals.

By October 1977, however, only five years after lot sales began, all 3,054 residential building sites had been sold or spoken for. Ray and Bill Watt's direct involvement in the development of SDCE was essentially done.

The foundation for a great community had been established — the rest was up to the people who would call San Diego Country Estates home.

People Are
The Community

RAY WATT DID SOMETHING UNIQUE when he developed San Diego Country Estates — he deeded all the amenity improvements to the property owners. That list included the golf course, clubhouse with bar and restaurant, swimming pool and tennis courts, the 30-unit guest lodge, two equestrian centers and Ramona Oaks Park. All of these facilities came with their underlying land and open space corridors, amounting to more than 1,300 acres of common area.

Forming property owners' associations to accept and maintain common areas is not unusual in California real estate developments. What is exceptional, however, is that when the San Diego Country Estates Association (SDCEA) came into being, it was immediately faced with operating a resort complex that employed dozens of people and grossed more than a million dollars in annual receipts. During the early years of development, this responsibility was largely carried by Watt's management team.

As more people moved into the community, the board

of directors of the association evolved from a developer-dominated body to what it is today, an independent nonprofit corporate board. A sound organizational and physical foundation had been put in place. It was recognized that the needs of a growing community, such as ours, would require dedicated and capable volunteer directors and professional management. It would also require that the association be a good partner with various local governmental agencies.

Building on Watt's Infrastructure

While Watt built all the basic infrastructure and amenities, he knew that additional improvements would be needed as the community grew and added new homes. Being primarily a lot sales program, not a housing tract, individual property owners would determine the actual pace of future development. The building-out of more than 3,400 dwelling units would dictate the timing of when additional public facilities and improvements would be needed. And as the local government's income increased with the property tax base and service fees generated from SDCE's growth, it was expected that public improvements would keep pace with those demands.

It was planned that treated effluent from our reclaimed water plant would be used to irrigate the San Vicente Golf Course. The original plant that was built provided capacity to service the first thousand homes. Its foundation was designed and built to accommodate future incremental expansion. Effluent disposal for the first few years was done with spray fields next to the plant. When in 1981, the flows were soon reaching the capacity of those fields,

RAMONA OAKS PARK in 2013, with the children's playground in the foreground, and the covered picnic area with the pavilion in the background on the left.

and the volume was large enough to justify building a system to pipe the reclaimed water back up to the golf club, neither the Ramona Municipal Water District (RMWD) nor SDCEA had enough capital to fund those improvements.

The Solk Ranch located on Spangler Mountain (later sold and renamed Spangler Peak Ranch) offered to buy the treated effluent to irrigate their avocado grove. They agreed to build piping, pumping and storage to their grove in return for the "wastewater" at a reduced rate. Their contract was for 10 years, and it was seen as an expedient way to buy time. This limited commitment gave both private/public parties more time to prepare for building the needed improvements to deliver treated water on the golf course, and it saved having to acquire and build additional spray fields.

In 1999, our association spent $1 million to modernize our golf course irrigation system to receive the expected reclaimed water. In 2003, another $1 million of ratepayers' money (SDCE property owners) was spent by the water district to construct a transmission line from the treatment plant to the golf course.

The avocado grower's initial contract had been extended by the RMWD to run until December 2008. All of this cheap water was guaranteed to him with a proviso that he release any water he didn't need to SDCE. However, less than 10% of the annual plant production of 600 acre feet was ever released. From 2004 through 2007, our water costs were increasing at a rate of 25% to 30% a year. Enough was enough.

In anticipation of the expiration of the contract between the water district and the grower in 2008, the SDCEA Board of Directors formed an ad hoc committee to study the situation and work out a plan for getting more of this water. The committee, led by Ernest Garrett and Maggie Johnson, conducted extensive studies, which confirmed that SDCE was entitled to a greater share of the plant's output and could handle it.

In 2008 a new three-way, 10-year contract was negotiated between the water district, the grower and the association to assure a more equitable distribution of the water. Three lakes on the golf course, on holes one, three and 18, were enlarged, increasing our overall storage capacity by 63%, and greatly enhancing the beauty of the course. And using reclaimed water saved the golf course $1.5 million in purchases of potable water just during the period of 2011 and 2012. This tremendous accomplishment was thanks to the work of that ad hoc team, since renamed the standing Committee on Water Resource Management. The current chairman of the committee is Don Shumacher.

Association's Growing Pains

While the transition from a developer to a member-run operation was rocky at times in those early years, it was, however, relatively smooth when put in the perspective of time, and of the magnitude and complexities of the many factors involved. This success was to the credit of developers Bill and Ray Watt who gave much of their energy and heavily subsidized operational losses during those formative years of 1973 through 1977. It is also to the credit of those dedicated and capable members on the association board, who served long hours without pay.

However, by 1980, it became apparent that operational losses, especially in the restaurant and resort, were becoming excessively burdensome for the fledgling association. The board was reluctant to increase assessments and instead opted to lease the bar, restaurant and lodge to an outside hotel operator. That arrangement failed, lasting less than two years. After experiencing these disappointing results, the board of directors resumed direct control of management and operation. But that experience proved costly in more ways than one and nearly caused us to lose our state liquor license.

However, in 2006 the association again revisited the possibility of contracting out operation of the restaurant and bar. A survey was sent to the membership to get their opinion about such a change, and the results were mixed. Negotiations, however, were started with a local restaurateur and reached a serious level before that effort was finally dropped. The board decided instead to make a stronger effort at improving our self-operation.

A new food and beverage manager, Debbie Warren, was brought on to improve quality and service, and Joyce Whelehon was appointed to generate more group promotions, banquets and wedding parties. The clubhouse facilities received major remodeling, with the redecorating of the restaurant, a major renovation of the bar and lounge, and the addition of an outside patio dining area.

The changes have greatly transformed that side of the association's business, and have raised hope that those operations, which have been a source of constant frustration, have taken on a new direction.

Association Board and Management

From April 1973, when the first annual meeting was held, until early 2013 — a span of four decades — 66 members have served on the SDCE Association Board of Directors. A list of those directors, and the years they served, can be found in an appendix in the back of this book. These men and ladies, who come from all walks of life and professional backgrounds, continue to serve, receiving no remuneration for their services.

Over these years, the association's facilities and

operations have been run by several general managers. John and Sally Morrison were the first. They did a most capable and congenial job while working under chaotic conditions during the land sales promotion period from 1972 to 1977, when half the clubhouse served as a sales pavilion and the other half as a bar and restaurant. Managers who followed included Hank Litten, Fred Harris, Hal Gansert. Gordon Cairnes, Bill Jacobs, Sheldon Osborn and Fred Stoner. Since the 1990s, the general managers have been Dennis Damon (1993), C. David Waite (1993-94), Al Powers (1994-2000), Bob Mariani (2000-01), Bob Harchut (2001-05) and Al Powers again in 2005. The man presently serving since 2005 is Mario Trejo.

Pioneer Homeowners

It took real pioneer spirit to move into SDCE in the 1973-75 period, before all the improvements were complete and when neighbors were few and far between. Those who did had a vision of how their community would develop and were willing to put up with the hardships that they knew would be only temporary.

Some of those early residents who stand out as part of the first hundred homeowner pioneers include Hubbard and Diana Lynch. Diana spent long hours organizing social events for her neighbors. Ray and Mary Ann Balwierczak were the first permanent residents in the first condo phase. Other pioneers include Rex and Jean Blewett, Ralph and Bette Thompson, Joe and Pat Rayburn and Dorothy Moses. Ramona general practitioner, Dr. John and wife Louise DeKock were the first to build on the golf course. Others included Bob and Rose Wilcoxen, Ken and Pauline Smith, and Leo and Edith Elizalde.

Prominent among SDCE commercial pathfinders were Paul and Dorothy Whelehon, who took a gamble and started the Village Store in early 1977 when just a handful of people lived in the valley. The commitment paid off well for them, as well as for the many who have enjoyed its convenience. Other pioneers who provided early service in the valley were Jack and Margie Gamberg, who opened San Vicente's first dry cleaning and tailoring shop.

The Whelehons and Gambergs subsequently sold these businesses, but today the footprint of this commercial center remains much as it did in 1977. In the meantime, the population in SDCE has grown more than six-fold. While there was talk by a new owner who bought the center, with its 14-acre commercial site, of expanding with more shops, larger stores and a service station, no significant facility changes have taken place since. A new major retail enterprise was added, however, to replace a health club that had closed. In 2011, SDCE homeowner Jeff Fabian, with partner Ralph Peebler, opened a full-service Ace Hardware and Garden Center, adding a much-needed service and convenience for the community.

The popular and improved Java Hut, at the front of the center, has been owned and operated by Bob Murray since 2007. Country Wine and Liquor (formerly called the Village Store), which has been significantly enhanced, has been owned and operated by Shawn Kattoula since 2005.

PIONEER SDCE MERCHANTS Paul Whelehon (left), the original proprietor of the Village Store, and Jack Gamberg, the first owner of San Vicente Cleaners, are pictured in 1982.

MODERN-DAY OPERATORS Bob Murray (left), owner of the Java Hut, is shown with neighbor merchant Shawn Kattoula, owner of the Country Wine and Liquor Village Store.

Environmental Control

Home building in SDCE, as it was originally intended, has been an individual matter. Homes are designed and built by individual lot owners.

With the objective of protecting property values and ensuring that these various designs harmonize with the setting and with community desires, an Environmental Control Committee (ECC) was set up to review and approve all building plans.

A set of broad controls were established in a Declaration of Covenants, Conditions and Restrictions by the developer before any lots were sold. These CC&Rs were recorded and are part of each property owner's title.

The ECC is appointed by the association's board and is responsible for upholding the CC&Rs. Those who have devoted their service to the committee during the years of rapid growth include George Marty, John DeKock, Jim Flagg, Rex Blewett, Bill Watt, George Palmer, John Frazier, Jim Barnes, Charlie Marsh, Dick Barber, Robert Wheeler, Desmond Partridge, Ken Strain, Don Sweet, Clyde Jackson, Bill Fenton and Jack Mikesel.

In recent years, those who've served for more than a year, in this seemingly thankless job, have been Mike Cassidy, Charlie Brown, Jim McGuire, Ed Anderson, Dave Chamberlin and, Donald Olson.

Early Growth Rate

San Diego Country Estates experienced steady growth during its first 10 years. During the real estate boom of 1977-79, ECC construction approvals ran at the healthy rate of 8 to 10 new homes each month. But this expansion was nothing to compare with what happened during the 1980s. At the time this book was first published in February 1983, there were a total of about 800 single family homes and 375 condos in place. By November 1990, that total had grown to nearly 2,300 single family and 385 condominium homes. The specific plan for SDCE was more than 75% built-out by 1997.

The biggest SDCE boom in construction occurred during the period from 1986 through 1988. The ECC approved plans at an average rate of 25 homes per month in 1986, 34 per month in 1987 and 23 in 1988.

All this time the Ramona Municipal Water District was collecting sewer fees for these houses and had amassed a capital improvement fund of more than $4 million for expansion of the wastewater treatment plant. However, while accumulating this fund, they had failed to keep pace with the growth. The District imposed a building moratorium due to lack of plant capacity in late 1988. It lasted the better part of two years, putting a damper on home construction. The ban was finally lifted in August 1990 as construction of the long overdue plant expansion neared completion.

Golf

To a considerable degree, social life in SDCE has revolved around sports and recreation. The largest organized groups have been the men's and ladies' golf clubs. During the first few years the San Vicente Golf Course was open, in 1973-75, golf association dues were $15 monthly, yet the San Vicente Golf Club was doing well to have but 25 paid family memberships. The club's membership hit a high point of 426 in 2005, which contrasts sharply with 270 today in 2013. Much of this decline can be attributed to a greater proportion of younger working families in our association's demographics and to recent economic uncertainties.

During the formative years, the San Vicente Golf Club (SVGC) presidents were Harvard Noble (1973-75) and Donald LeRoux (1975-77), and the San Vicente Women's Golf Association (SVWGA) was headed by Winnie Peterson (1973-74), Nancy LeMenager (1975) and Mary Ann Balwierczak (1976).

SVGC presidents who followed were Holland Hilton (1977-79), Bob Faulkner and Ed Breznyak (1980), Bob Ryrholm and Bill Nelson (1981), John Everett (1982), Flip Rodine (1983), Dale Bratten (1984-85), Dan Cross (1986), Bill Breckwoldt (1987), Jim Lewis (1988), Norb Kluewer (1989) and John Mallon (1990).

The current SVGC president is Jim Munsterman, who was preceded by Jerry Daniels (2009-10), David Greenwood (2008), Don Mizaur (2007), Don Schumacher (2004-06), Jack Knowles (2003), Lynn Abernathy (2002), Ernest Garrett (2001), Wally Kuebler, (1998 and 2000) and Ed Morrison (1999). The only woman to hold this position was Barbara Marty, in 1997.

Early SVWGC presidents included Nancy Miller and Billie Harper (1978), Addie Quick (1979), Lucy Hechter (1980), Margaret Blyth (1981), Helen Johnson (1982), Billie Johns (1983), Barbara Graham (1984), Pat Heath (1985), Nancy Smith (1986), Joyce Durand (1987), Jo Boyer (1988), LaNora Lauritzen (1989) and Joyce Whitehead (1990).

SAN VICENTE GOLF CLUB MEMBERS get ready for their shotgun start at the 2013 annual couples' Valentine Day Tournament.

THE 18th TEE at San Vicente Golf Course is shown with the enlarged lake and new waterfall feature added in 2011.

They were followed by Rachael Gilmore, Shirley Tilsen, Pat Fenton, Barbara Marty, Marge Randall, Judy Wineland, Margaret Stranigan, Carol Harvigsen, Pat Harrisberger, Mary Lou Kohl, Kathy Hunter, Lorraine Schnell, Grace Fendrich, Virginia Pollack, Marie Hamann, Judy Mizaur, Jo Barefoot, Florine Murillo, Sharon Mowry, Phyllis Neilson, Karen Elston and Shauna Porter.

The current (2013) SVWGA president is Maureen Greenwood.

— *Tournaments & Social Events*

The ladies' and men's annual calendar reads like a cornucopia of social and serious competitive golf. Set events range from the women's weekly Tuesday and men's regular formal Wednesday tournaments, to the special days when each group manages to carve out six to 10 starting times each Thursday for the women and Friday for the men. In other words, members in good standing can usually find a game with their same gender at least twice a week without any trouble.

The men have a senior team and regular club golf team that play similar groups from other clubs in the region, as do the women.

Couples' member tournaments are held once a month with different themes. Each has their annual president's cup and club champion tournaments. There is a member-member, as well as a member-guest tournament each year. The women's big affair is their annual Pow-Wow tourney usually held each May. The men's big one is their member-guest match in June. A couple's dinner dance is held twice a year, with the Christmas party highlighting the calendar.

NUMBER 13 FAIRWAY, where pioneers once grew barley and ruins of the Mykrantz dairy were cleared when the golf course was built, is shown in the shadow of Spangler Peak. Teeing off in 1974 is Nancy LeMenager, one of the first presidents of the San Vicente Women's Golf Association.

— *Professional Golf Staff*

The San Vicente golf program has had seven PGA professionals in charge. Chuck Jones was the first to take over in 1972, before the course officially opened for play the following February, and he provided considerable support for the fledgling club. When Chuck left in 1981, his assistant, Bruce Stevens, became head pro. Others who have held this position include Terry Horn, Bob Harchut, Greg Pruden, Mark Hayden and since 2005, John Rathbun.

The first golf course superintendent, Fred Harris, who helped build San Vicente Golf Course, moved on to help Ray Watt build the Fairbanks Ranch course in 1982. He was succeeded by his assistant, Ken Sommermeyer, who held the position for 14 years. Pat Shannon, hired in 1991, was his assistant until 1996 when he was appointed superintendent of golf course and open space maintenance. He has served in that position since.

— *Junior Golf*

Our pro shop has been in the forefront of promoting junior golf ever since 1989, when a summer clinic was first started with just 15 enrollees. By 1991, 92 youngsters had signed up for this annual summer event. It has continued to be a strong program since under the fine direction of Fred Arcaina, our assistant golf professional.

— *San Vicente's LPGA Champ*

John and Marion Mallon retired here from Michigan in the mid-1980s while daughter, Megan, was attending Ohio State University and active in several sports programs. After her folks moved here, Meg adopted San Vicente and Ramona as her home, and later let the world know it. She went on to become a champion member of the Ladies Professional Golf Association's (LPGA) tour.

Many of the folks here watched her progress as she climbed up the rankings to become one of the top women's

POW-WOW IS THE LADIES BIG INVITATIONAL GOLF EVENT. Shown at their 10th annual tournament held in September 1989 are members (from left, back row) Jo Ann Brink, Jo Boyer, Colleen Barnum, Bettie Knight, Rachael Gilmore and LaNora Lauritzen and (front row) Betty Lou Zimmerman, Dori Stansberry, Vicky Lukacs and Lois Nass.

golfers in the world. Her fan club here, "Meg's Mob," followed her to many tournaments as she advanced in the pro ranks right into her crowning year when she won two major events in a three-week period. The summer of 1991 saw Meg win the 37th LPGA Championship at Bethesda, Md., and the U.S. Women's Open at Fort Worth, Texas.

Tennis

The Riggs-Court match drew a lot of international attention to tennis, and that fact wasn't lost on SDCE developer Ray Watt. We set out to pick a site and get our county government land-use plan changed to allow for a stand-alone tennis facility. Watt had one designed and built across from Ramona Oaks Park in little over a year. It was to be a first-class resort operation and tennis school. He talked to world champion, Rod Laver, "the Rocket," who was operating another one in Southern California to see if Rod would be interested in bringing his program to San Vicente. They worked out a deal, but not before Rod insisted that Ray build it with 20 courts, which he did. There are not many 20-court tennis camps in California, but we have one, and that's the reason. Laver operated a popular program employing 10, to as many as 20, instructors from 1975 through 1976.

Subsequent tennis schools included the World Junior Tennis Academy (WJTA), from 1981 to 1989, which was a full-time program where most of the 50 to 60 young attendees lived in the valley and attended Ramona High School. The academy was started by Ian Russell and later by Mark Berner. The Chuck Boyle Academy followed into the 1990s.

The facility started off being called the San Vicente Tennis Ranch, then Racquet Club, and then Ramona Canyon Club. After being purchased by the Riviera Oaks Resorts, its current name is Riviera Oaks Resort and Racquet Club.

Some of the early SDCEA member tennis activists and organizers were Marge Boone Askin, Gurdon and Jane

STARTING THEM YOUNG. Tennis pro Katrina Failla works with 5- to 8-year-olds at one of the SDCEA Recreation Department's tennis clinics that are run by Greg and Katrina Failla.

Henry, Lynn and Fred Riffle, actor Ross Martin, Bill Edwards, Barbara Paige, Cecil Girdlestone and Candy Joslin.

Tennis activity has remained strong at the two venues available to property owners. They can use the four courts next to the golf course free of extra cost, and Riviera Oaks is open for outsiders to join, offering memberships at moderate fees.

Both centers see a variety of activities and organized programs, in addition to casual play. While the four association courts at the main clubhouse are under the control of SDCEA and have seen limited league and team play, they nevertheless get plenty of use from individual members and guests and from the various programs and clinics conducted by tennis pros Greg Failla and wife, Katrina. Both are former junior and collegiate champions and nationally ranked players. In addition to after-school tennis clinics, they offer individual instruction and conduct special summer and year-round camps for youth. One is a unique three-hour instructional program that features one hour of tennis, one of golf and one of swimming.

Riviera Oaks Club is a beehive of activity today with nearly 100 of its lady members active in five different women's area leagues. The club's pro is Doug Failla, Greg's brother, also a former collegiate champion, who operates independently of SDCEA's recreation program. Doug conducts clinics and member tournaments, offers individual tennis instruction, and has been coach of the Ramona High School tennis team for more than six years. The team works out and plays their home matches there.

The two brothers got their introduction to San Vicente Valley when, as youth, they moved to Ramona in 1981, enrolling and graduating from the WJTA.

Recreation Volunteers

Originally, the many association recreation programs and special events were run by volunteers, but that work developed into a semi-fulltime job during the 1980s. The first to take on this responsibility was Joan Gansert in 1981, followed by Pam Willis in 1984. But volunteers were still largely responsible for organizing community

FOURTH OF JULY IN SDCE. The Kerri Lane "choo-choo" float won first place in the 1988 annual parade. The parade and picnic in Ramona Oaks Park have been a popular tradition for more than 35 years.

picnics and other activities, such as the annual Fourth of July parade and picnic in Ramona Oaks Park, with games and amusement booths. Volunteers ran the events and prepared and served refreshments. In one year, 1987, according to association leader Marlene Robershaw, more than 1,600 hot dogs were served at the picnic.

Because of member demands for more recreation facilities and equipment, the association board decided in 1987 to form a Recreation Advisory Committee. It was composed of representatives from the different geographical areas of the community, as well as various activity groups requiring association support. Among those who played key leadership roles were Diane Schafer, John Marciano, Tom Larkin, Lee Brown, Joyce

Whitehead, Mike Minor, Jerrie Raymer, Bob Hailey and O.G. "Bud" Fais.

One of the many products of this committee's efforts was a long-range master recreation plan, which was developed to assist the association board in addressing future needs. Some of their recommendations, like a new clubhouse and the addition of another pool, proved financially infeasible for the time being.

However, their recommendation for additional small parks was picked up in 2008 when the recreation committee was revived after a period of dormancy. As a result, a new pocket park was developed on Gunn Stage Way, in addition to a pocket park with dog runs on Bassett Way and another dog park in Ramona Oaks Park. Current members of the recreation committee include Bill Fox, Breeanna Purcell, Elizabeth Trausch, Sharon Ferguson and the author.

Recreation Department

Programs and activities were added over the years to the point that a recreation department with a professional staff and full-time director was formally established in 1995 with Sherry Yardley as its first director.

The current director of the department, Julie Perreault, has headed up their multi-faceted programs since 1997. They also run and supervise two swimming pools, Ramona Oaks Park and the two pocket parks. The department manages contract sports programs, such as tennis, community event vendors, concerts in the park and members' tours.

Their activities range from a preschool for tots to field

excursions for seniors. Ongoing events include after-school programs for kids, early-riser classes for adults and concerts at the pavilion. They also offer swim lessons during the day, movies by the pool in the evening, summer campouts and car shows. Members need only refer to the monthly listings in the San Vicente Valley News to learn about the recreational opportunities. Each program is self-sustaining for the most part, and new activities are added as enough demand develops.

Equestrian Activities

It is evident today that the horse environment provided in SDCE has been well accepted by valley horse lovers, and it is considered one of the best equestrian communities in the West.

Today it is estimated that the horse population in SDCE numbers nearly 500. These include more than 300 that are kept on homeowners' lots, plus those quartered at our two centers.

Today our International Equestrian Center's (IEC) original eight barns are fully occupied. To that have been added 38 corrals and a 'mare hotel.' The total number of horses being housed and cared for there by their owners is about 100.

The Casey Tibbs Western Center has four barns. One of them is reserved for trail horses. Riviera Oak Resort rents the barn, offering trail rides in our eastern end of the San Vicente Valley for members and guests. The four barns and 60 corrals at the center house about 80 horses.

Both equestrian centers are supervised by the association's equestrian director, Teri Zaffarano.

217

Activities centered at the IEC include the San Vicente Saddle Club's trail rides, progressive breakfasts, barbecues, poker runs and such. The Pony Club was one of the first organizations formed by property owners and has remained active for all these many years. They hold regular local events, as well as regional competitions. Other activities include combined tests, dressage and gymkhana shows.

And as with the other facilities, it has taken work and enthusiasm on the part of individual property owners to create and promote activities to fully capitalize on their potential. Property owners who initially laid out trails and helped organize resident equestrian activities include Dick and Carol Shimer, Joe and Pat Rayburn, Ted Hall and Reno Harnish.

Subsequently, with the increase in horse population, the Saddle Club has greatly expanded under the leadership of past club presidents Larry Bazinet, Tom Garibay, Gwen Pellecchia, John Royer and Reno Harnish. Current president, Randy MacRostie, has led the group for the past 10 years.

The International Equestrian Center was also home to trainers and show people Budd and Mary Boetticher, and Linda Campbell-Abbott. Hunter-jumper and dressage shows, cross-country and Pony Club events, Lusitano exhibitions and the training of race horses are all part of the history and facility's ongoing scene. Pony Club pioneer leaders included Capt. Joe Rayburn, Marguerite Tudor, Carol Rigdon, Belle Bohm and Nora Milner. The SDCEA Pony Club is still active, having combined with the club in Ramona.

A MEMORIAL GROVE at Ramona Oaks Park playground honors departed members of the San Vicente Valley Club. Past club presidents Judy Nachazel (left) and Peggy Rice are shown in February 1986, putting finishing touches on the project to provide more shade and beauty in the park.

San Vicente Valley Club

In 1980, Jay Vork and Margaret Kempenaar spearheaded the formation of a newcomers' club that has developed into a driving force in the whole Ramona community. Beginning with less than a dozen interested women, the San Vicente Valley Club now boasts more than 100 members. The organization is now commonly referred to as the Valley Club, since membership is no longer limited to only those residing in our valley, but is open to other Ramona area women, as well.

While the club provides an opportunity for meeting neighbors and making new friends, their monthly meetings offer interesting programs. The group can best be described as a civic and community service organization. The long list of worthy local causes and programs that they generously support grows each year. Their big fundraising event is the annual home tour, which raises money for their charitable work. Projects that have benefited include Ramona High School scholarships, the Food and Clothes Closet and SDCE pool and park equipment, among many others.

Ladies who have served as president were pioneers: Margaret Kempenaar (1980), Ann Haywood (1981), Bonnie Mang (1982), Jean Wickham (1983), Judy Ploughe (1984), Anita Ryrholm and Marguerite Tudor (1985), Kay Bray (1986), Judy Nachazel (1987), Rita Nicolaides (1988), Peggi Rice (1989) and Carolyn Harms (1990).

In more recent years, the presidents have included Eileen Castberg, Connie Phillips, Maggie Johnson, Nancy Frazee, Shirley Leyrer, Karen Clendenen, Peggie Rice, Helen Johnson Jupin, Kaaren Thiem, Patty Payne and Joan Renaud.

Schools

When the master plan was approved for SDCE in the early 1970s, three sites were reserved for future school construction. By the early 1980s, plans were well underway by the Ramona Unified School District for construction of San Vicente Valley's first school. Fittingly, the first school, which was dedicated in September 1985, was named in honor of James Dukes, one of the valley's early pioneers and a long-time Ramona school trustee.

James Dukes Elementary School is located on Abalar Way in Unit V of SDCE. Its first principals were Karen Clark, David Wilson and Joseph Annicharico.

JAMES DUKES ELEMENTARY SCHOOL, the first school built in the estates, is shown on a typical busy afternoon.

RECOGNIZED AS A TOP SCHOOL. Barnett Elementary School, located in the estates, received a California State Distinguished School Award in 2012.

THE SCIENCE OLYMPIAD TEAM from James Dukes Elementary School scored well in competition with youngsters from schools throughout the county. This 1988 competition was held at Point Loma College.

By September 1990, enrollment had exceeded 900 students and the valley was clearly overdue for another facility. Barnett Elementary School opened its doors for the first time in September 1992. It is located in Unit II between Arena Drive and Del Amo Road on one of those original master-planned sites. The school is named in honor of Augustus and Martha Barnett, early San Vicente Valley pioneers and Ramona Town Hall benefactors.

Today (in 2013), enrollment at the two schools stands at 535 at James Dukes and 495 at Barnett.

Religious Congregations
While Rancho San Vicente has had a permanent Roman Catholic Church since 1933, located on the Indian Reservation in Barona Valley, the San Vicente

MR. AND MRS. SANTA CLAUS come to visit the children in San Vicente in 1989. Mitzie and Lee Brown enjoyed this event, along with the kiddies, for more than five years.

PRESENT DAY SANTA AND MRS. CLAUS, David and Eileen Castberg, arrive in a carriage.

Valley has yet to see its first church building constructed. With about 10,000 people residing in SDCE, and the fact that no permanent places of worship have been built here, most San Vicente residents attend services at religious congregations in Ramona.

The Reform Congregation Etz Chaim, however, which comprises about 25 families, continues to meet in the Rotunda at the International Equestrian Center, as it has since 1981. Services are conducted by Rabbi Leslie Bergson and Rabbi Ben Leinow. The congregation president currently is Dianna Levin, who succeeded Marvin and Rhoda Hamburger.

San Vicente Valley News

The valley got its first full-fledged newspaper when the SDCE Association board decided the membership was entitled to receive better communication and more complete news about their community. In 1988, several board members, especially Godfrey Tudor-Matthews and the author, felt the association had an obligation to see that a real newspaper was available for the members, and that the association should commit to publishing one, if necessary. In early 1988, Laura Brien and Chuck LeMenager organized the San Vicente Valley News, and two years later the paper was recognized and accepted as a full-fledged member of the California Newspaper Publisher's Association.

Continuously published by the SDCE Association for 30 years, it is distributed to more than 3,200 member families without charge. So far, the monthly tabloid, averaging 32 pages per issue, has been substantially self-

CUTTING THE CAKE in March 1990 to celebrate the second birthday of the San Vicente Valley News are some who had a hand in that paper's early success. Shown are (from left) Pam Torregrosa, advertising; Fred Stoner, association manager; Laura Brien, manager/first editor; Guy Brien, production, and Cheryl Manno, advertising.

sufficient from advertising revenues.

In making the decision in 1988 to publish the paper, the association board determined they wanted a real newspaper, not a 'house organ.' Editorial content and letters to the editor, in good taste, are published regardless of whether or not they agree with current board politics or actions. Editors who followed Brien, when she retired after two years here, were Virgil Bradshaw, a SDCE homeowner and former Associated Press executive; Judy Nachazel; Sandy Cole, and Janice Baldridge.

The editorial board is currently comprised of editor Janice Baldridge, SDCEA General Manager Mario Trejo, Don Mizaur, Judy Nachazel, Beth Edwards, Doug Kafka and the author.

APPENDIX
Directors, SDCE Association

William Watt 1973-79

Charles LeMenager............ 1973-79,
    1987-90, 2008-09, 2012-13

John DeKock 1973-78

C.G. "Gus" Pappas.............. 1973-75

Fred Harris........................ 1973-74

Harvard Noble 1974-77

George Marty..................... 1975-78

Townsend King 1977-80

Hans Schiff 1978-80

Arno Muller 1978-79

Nadine Anderson 1979-82

Ashley Orr......................... 1979-80

Robert Bowen 1980-81

John Aguero 1980-81

Gordon Cairnes..........................1980

Ralph Thompson.......................1980

Paul Champion 1980-83

Ray Balwierczak 1980-83

Lee Chamberlin................... 1981-84

Kenneth Heath.................... 1981-84

Wilmer Mitchell................. 1982-85

John Vork........................... 1982-85

Sam Myrick........................ 1983-86

C.J. "Flip" Rodine 1984-87

Martin Elenbaas 1984-89

Alton Watson 1985-88

O.G. "Bud" Fais................. 1985-88

Godfrey Tudor-Matthews 1986-89

Charles Marsh 1987-90

Larry Porter........................ 1988-90

Lewis Weinberg................... 1989-92

Jerrie Raymer 1989-93

Robert Reich 1990-93

Pat Kroncke........................ 1990-94

J. Perry Jones 1990-94,
    2006-08, 2012-13

John Harms........................ 1992-95

Don Sweet.......................... 1993-96

Connie Bull.......... 1993-99, 2006-09

Ron Feederle 1994-2001

Bill Fox..................... 1994-97, 2009

Stan Sewitch............................1996

Jim Spencer 1997-99, 2001-02

Marlene Robershaw......... 1997-2000

Mark Johnson 1998-2001

Judi DePuy...................... 1999-2001

Armando Montes 2000-01

Gary Jahrig..............................2001

Vern Hazen 2001-06

Robert Argyelan 2001-04

Dick Bender 2002-06

Pam Howes 2003-04

Al Riedler 2004-06

Will Krutz.......................... 2003-05

Maggie Johnson 2005, 2012-13

Dusty Brown....................... 2006-07

Gary Tiegs...............................2006

Al Powers 2007

Eileen Castberg 2006-13

NOTE: The terms and the method of electing the five-member San Diego Country Estates Association Board of Directors were established by the developer and were the standard that was followed for more than two decades. Terms were to be three years for all board members. However, in order to achieve a degree of board and program continuity in future years, at the initial election, held in 1973, each of the five who won that year drew straws to serve staggered terms. Two of them were to serve three years, two for two years and one for one year. All subsequent elections were to set terms for all board seats at three years.

That three-year standard worked well for more than 23 years until it was challenged in court and changed by a judges' ruling in 1996. Three members had sued the association to change the standard system to a "three, two or one" year term. The court held in favor of the challengers. All incumbent directors were removed and at the next and all subsequent elections, each seat was defined as either a one-, two- or three-year term.

ACKNOWLEDGMENTS

There were many people who helped with this book. We wish to acknowledge and extend our sincere thanks to them.

To Ray Watt for introducing us to this beautiful area. To Guy Woodward and his Ramona Pioneer Historical Society Museum for providing a wealth of local historical information and photos. To Joe Welch, Josephine Romero, Catherine Welch and other members of the Barona Tribal Council for their valuable help and photos. To Title Insurance and Trust Company for access to their title abstracts for the rancho. To Richard Pourade for his fine books and for access to some of his notes. To Sylvia Arden, Jane and Larry Booth and the San Diego Historical Society. To Jim Moriarty and Brian Smith of the University of San Diego for their input on the early Indians. To Herbert Klein for the helping hand at Copley Newspapers. To Jim Barnett, Dorace and June Scarbery, and Sam Quincey for their valuable assistance. To the courteous and helpful staffs at the Federal Archives and Record Center and the California Room at the San Diego Public Library. Last but not least, what could anyone do without family and relatives? Many thanks to my journalist son Jack, for his assistance, and to my sister Donna and brother-in-law Ernie Prinzhorn for their contributions.

The final phase of this project, the "Revisited" edition, was a major effort. The wrap-up of previous editions, and addition of much new material, wouldn't have gone as professionally nor as smoothly as it did without the fine organization and graphics work of Beth Edwards and the editing of Rose Marie Scott-Blair.

PHOTOS AND ILLUSTRATIONS

Sources of the photographs, graphics and artwork are listed alphabetically with page numbers. Those not listed were produced by the author. Bancroft Library, University of California, 65; Barona Indian Tribal Council Collection, 36, 38, 39; Laura Brien, 175 (top), 211, 222, 223 (top); Guy Brien, 219; Country Reporter, 167 (top and bottom); Leslie A. Dodd, 170, 176 (top), 185, 189; Beth Edwards, [x], [xi], 99, 165; Los Angeles Times, 172; James Robert Moriarty Collection, 18, 19; Mary Ann Pentis, 173, 176 (top and bottom), 189, 215; Ernest Prinzhorn, Cover, 67; Ramona Pioneer Historical Society, 27, 63, 111, 118, 121, 123, 125, 126, 127, 128, 129, 155; Ramona Town Hall Collection, 113; San Diego Historical Society, 70; San Diego Historical Society – Title Insurance & Trust Collection, 90, 106, 133, 136, 159; San Diego Union, 44, 105; San Vicente Valley News, 175 (bottom), and June Mykrantz Scarbery Collection, 141, 147.

REFERENCES

Bancroft, Hubert Howe. 1886. *History of California,* VOls. III, V & VII. San Francisco: The History Company, Publishers.

Barnett, Augustus. 1882-90. Accounts Ledger. Collection: Ramona Pioneer Historical Society.

Barnett, James M. 1980-82. Interview. Ramona. By author.

Brackett, R.W. 1939. *History of San Diego County Ranchos.* San Diego: Title Insurance & Trust Co.

Burkhart, Lark. 3/6/80. *Old Times, Tall Tales & Fond Memories.* Ramona Sentinel.

Cauzza, Victor. 1982. Interview. Santa Ysabel. By author.

Country Reporter, The. 1972-78. The San Diego Country Estates, property owner newsletter. San Diego Estates Co.

Crosby, Harry W. 1981. *Last of the Californios.* La Jolla, Calif.: The Copley Press, Inc.

Daley, Carlyle M. 1960. Interview, San Diego. By Edgar F. Hastings. Collection: San Diego Historical Society.

Davidson, Winifred. Notes on early San Diego Genealogy. Collection: San Diego Historical Society.

Davis, William Heath. 1929. *Seventy-five Years in California.* San Francisco: John Howell.

Dukes, James. 1959. Interview, Ramona. By Edgar F, Hastings. Collection: San Diego Historical Society.

Dumke, Glenn S. 1940. *The Boom of the Eighties in Southern California.* San Marino: Henry E. Huntington Library & Art Gallery.

Elliott, A.B. 1980. Interview, Ramona. By author.

Engstrand, Iris H.W. 1980. *San Diego: California's Cornerstone.* Tulsa, OkIa.: Continental Heritage Press, Inc.

U.S. Federal Census, 1850 & 1860. Los Angeles & San Diego Counties.

Fletcher, Col. Ed. 1952. *Memoirs of Ed Fletcher.* San Diego: Pioneer Printers.

Head, Joseph. 1969. Capitan Grande. Personal memoirs.

Hill, Joseph J. 1927. *History of Warner's Ranch and Its Environs.* Los Angeles: privately printed.

Hughes, Charles. *The Decline of the Californios.* Master's Thesis: San Diego State University.

Indian Affairs, Office of; U.S. Dept. of Interior. 1931-48. Records and Reports, San Diego County Mission Indians, Laguna Niguel, Calif.: Federal Archives & Records Center.

Jackson, Helen Hunt. 1907. *A Century of Dishonor.* Boston: Little Brown & Company.

Kroeber, AL. 1953. *Handbook of the Indians of California.* Berkeley: California Book Co., Ltd.

Lands Commission, U.S. 1851-1873. Land grant claims, transcripts of hearings & court proceedings. Berkeley: Bancroft Library, University of California.

Merrill, Frederich J.H. 1913-14. 14th Report of the State Minerologist. California State Mining Bureau: Dec. 1914.

Meyer, LB. 8-1-1926. *Thar's Gold in Them Hills, Stranger.* San Diego Business Magazine.

Moore, Bertram B. 1956. *History of San Diego Roads and Stages.* Transcript: San Diego Historical Society.

Moretti, Ernest. 1982. Interview, Julian. By author.

Moriarty, James R. III. 1965. *Cosmogony Rituals, and Medical Practice Among The Diegueño Indians of Southern California.* Anthropological Journal of Canada, Vol. 3.

Moriarty, James R. III. *The Constant and Beautiful Valley.* Typescript: Ramona Pioneer Historical Society.

Mykrantz, John W. April 1927. *Indian Burials in Southern California.* Indian Notes: Vol. IV, No. 2, Museum of the American Indian, Heye Foundation, New York, N.Y.

Orange County California Genealogical Society. 1969. *Saddleback Ancestors.* Santa Ana, Calif.

Pourade, Richard F. 1961. *Time of the Bells.* San Diego Union-Tribune Publishing Co.

Pourade, Richard F. 1963. *The Silver Dons.* San Diego Union-Tribune Publishing Co.

Pourade, Richard F. 1966. *The Glory Years.* San Diego Union-Tribune Publishing Co.

Pourade, Richard F. 1965. *Gold in the Sun.* San Diego Union-Tribune Publishing Co.

Pourade, Richard F. 1967. *The Rising Tide.* San Diego Union-Tribune Publishing Co.

Pitt, Leonard. 1968. *The Decline of the Californios.* Berkeley & Los Angeles: University of California Press.

Quincey, Sam R. 1981. Interview, Ramona. By author.

Rensch, Hero Eugene. 1956. *Cullamac, Alias El Capitan Grande.* San Diego Historical Society Quarterly, Vol. 11, No. 3.

Richard, Luis M. May 10, 1936. *Report on the Geology of the Daley Mine, San Vicente Grant.* Ramona Pioneer Historical Society.

Richards, Rusty. 2010. *Casey Tibbs – Born to Ride,* Wickenberg, Ariz.: Moonlight Mesa Associates.

Robinson, W.W. 1948. Land in California. Berkeley: University of California Press.

Romero, Josephine. 1980. Interview, Barona Reservation. By author.

Rush Philip S. 1958. *History of the Californios.* San Diego.

Rush, Philip S. 1965. *Some Old Ranchos and Adobes.* San Diego.

San Diego County Board of Supervisors. 1882-88. Meetings, Minutes. Office of the Clerk of the Board.

San Diego County, Dept. of Public Works, road mapping division.

San Diego County Recorder. Property and Map Records.

San Diego County Tax Assessor. 1850-1869. Rancho assessment records. Collection: San Diego Historical Society.

San Diego Union. 1868-1973. Microfilms, San Diego Public Library.

Scarbery, Dorace E. 1981. Interview, Ramona. By author.

Scarbery, June Mykrantz. 1981. Interview, Ramona. By author.

Servin, Manuel P. 1973. *California's Hispanic Heritage: A View Into The Spanish Myth.* The Journal of San Diego History, S.D. Historical Society, Vol. XIX, No. 1.

Stephenson, Terry E. 1941. *Don Bernardo Yorbe.* Los Angeles.

Stockton, Louis Edward. 1958. Interview, Ramona. By Edgar F. Hastings. Collection: Ramona Pioneer Historical Society.

Stone, Irving. 1956. *Men to Match My Mountains.* Garden City, N.Y.: Doubleday & Company.

Thorne, Tanis C. 2012. *El Capitan.* Malki-Bellena Press, Banning, Calif.

Title Insurance & Trust Company. Abstract of title recordings for the Rancho Cañada de San Vicente y Mesa del Padre Barona, 1850-1962.

Title Insurance & Trust Company. Nov.-Dec. 1948 & Sept.-Oct. 1956. Ramona and the Santa Maria Valley, Ramona. Title Topics.

Valley, David J. 2003. *Jackpot Trail.* San Diego: Sunbelt Publications.

Waterman, Waldo D. 1958. Interview, San Diego. By Edgar F. Hastings. Collection: San Diego Historical Society.

Walters, Mary Dukes. 1974 & 1981. Interview, Escondido. By author.

Welch, Catherine. 1982. Interview, Barona Reservation. By author.

Welch, Edward "Joe." 2013. Interview, Barona Reservation. By author.

Woodward, Guy B. 1980-82. Interview, Ramona. By author.

INDEX

ABOUT THE AUTHOR

Charles LeMenager was, by profession, a land-use and planning consultant. Now, in semi-retirement, he spends more time with his avocations of researching and writing and community service.

He is a former executive with Fluor Corporation. Local and state government has also occupied much of his time, though mainly as a volunteer. He is a former mayor and councilman in the city of Santa Rosa, California, and was state director of housing and community development under Governor Ronald Reagan. Locally, he has served on the Ramona Municipal Water District board and the San Diego Country Estates (SDCE) Association board.

He came to Ramona in 1970 to help master plan and develop the new community of SDCE. He liked it so well, it's been his home ever since.

Other books by Mr. LeMenager include:

RAMONA AND ROUND ABOUT
A History of San Diego County's Little Known Back Country
Copyright 1989, 1990 and 1995, ISBN 0-9611102-2-8
Eagle Peak Publishing Company,
P.O. Box 1283, Ramona, California 92065

JULIAN CITY AND CUYAMACA COUNTRY
A History and Guide to the Past and Present
Copyright 1992, ISBN 0-911102-4-4
Eagle Peak Publishing Company

FLYING AFTER 50
You're Not Too Old to Start
Copyright 1995, ISBN 0-8138-2881-3
Iowa State University Press, Ames, Iowa 50014